COOKING IN THE
CANARY ISLANDS

AN ENCHANTING
JOURNEY THROUGH
THE SEVEN PEARLS

B BONECHI

HOW TO READ THE CARDS

DIFFICULTY	FLAVOR	NUTRITIONAL VALUE
● Easy	● Mild	● Low
●● Medium	●● Medium	●● Medium
●●● Difficult	●●● Strong	●●● High

Preparation and cooking times are shown in hours (h) and minutes (e. g. 30′ is 30 minutes).

Project: Casa Editrice Bonechi
Series editor: Alberto Andreini
Concept and texts: Paolo Piazzesi
Graphic design: Andrea Agnorelli and Maria Rosanna Malagrinò
Cover and layout: Maria Rosanna Malagrinò
Video layout for the English edition: Studio Grafico Vanni Berti
Editing: Maria Fiore Batini

English translation: Julia Weiss

Chef: Lisa Mugnai
Nutritionist: Dr. John Luke Hili

The photographs illustrating the recipes are the property of the Casa Editrice Bonechi Archives
and were taken by Andrea Fantauzzo.

Photographs of settings and scenery are the property of the Casa Editrice Bonechi Archives
and were taken by Marco Bonechi, Serena de Leonardis, Paolo Giambone.
*The publisher will be grateful for information concerning the sources of photographs
without credits and will be pleased to acknowledge them in future editions.*

© Copyright 2004
by CASA EDITRICE BONECHI, Florence - Italy
E-mail: bonechi@bonechi.it
Internet: www.bonechi.it
www.bonechi.com

Printed in Italy by Centro Stampa Editoriale Bonechi

ISBN 88-476-0948-8

***

A TABLE IN PARADISE

A bit of Europe in the middle of the Atlantic, at the same latitude as the Sahara Desert, a shred of Africa – or perhaps Atlantis – in Europe? The identity of the Canary Islands is truly a composite of myriad traditions and facets, created by the geographic location, by the generosity of nature that has blessed them in harmony with human endeavors, by their centuries-long role as a link between the Old and New Worlds before they were transformed into a vacation paradise. All this could not but be reflected in the archipelago's rich foods, that are quite eclectic as they combine the customs of mainland Spain with exotic ingredients, tropical foods with the cooking techniques and condiments of the temperate zones, and welcome suggestions from the Portuguese, Latin Americans and anyone who ever had dealings with the "Fortunate Islands" of the ancient world, without ever forgetting themselves. Canary Islands cooking, while open to any ideas or influence, resembles the land and people of the archipelago, reflecting both their parsimony, fantasy and love of the simple things that make for originality. It is a cult of customs that has developed into an ability to create delicious and surprisingly elegant dishes with things close at hand. They may take some effort, but they are unusual, home-style and genuine to the point that they even change the names, calling potatoes *papas* instead of the Spanish *patatas*, and turning *maiz* into *millo* for corn. Hierro, La Palma, Gomera, Tenerife, Gran Canaria, Fuerteventura and Lanzarote form a precious string of seven volcanic pearls that dot the ocean just above the Tropic of Capricorn, west of Morocco where African and Atlantic winds meet to create an enchanting climate. It is a magical place, and has been ever since the days of the Phoenician and Carthaginian navigators, even if only tireless efforts of the people – starting from the archipelago's first inhabitants, the *guanche* aborigines – have transformed it into the delightful garden that enchants us all. Here is Gran Canaria, known as the "little continent" because of its many environments, a green Mediterranean garden and orchard of exotic fruits; and the fertile islands that hold several records, Tenerife, with the tallest mountain in Spain, Pico de Teide that reaches to 3716 meters, and La Palma with the largest, active volcano in the world, Caldera de Taburiente that towers to nearly 2500 meters, the garden of the Canary Islands, famous for its sublime *malvasia*. And there is warm Fuerteventura, dotted with dunes, Lanzarote of the rolling hills, named for Lanzarotto Marocello who "rediscov-

Gran Canaria: details of the Cathedral of Santa Anna and the so-called House of Christopher Columbus in Las Palmas; above, the village of San Felipe.

ered" the archipelago in the thirteenth century after the Dark Ages; and the steep and rocky Gomera with the wild El Hierro, paradises of blissful solitude where human willpower won out over nature, to make outstanding wines.

This book contains the best of the recipes from these seven pearls, with all the most genuine traditional foods. As travelers fully know, tourist menus are one thing (even though there is more respect for traditions

here than in other places), local foods another. And it is our aim to acquaint you with the real foods of the Canary Islands, the exquisite recipes that have been handed down for generations, that offer delightful surprises for the palate and become another fond memory of an enchanting holiday (or an incentive to take one!). The foods are appetizing, plain and wholesome, based on natural ingredients, fla-

Tourists visiting the dunes of Maspalomas. Above, a potter at work.

vorful yet easy to digest. Rarely are there heavy ingredients (even though you should know that garlic abounds, and the variety that grows on the Islands is not for sissies); preparation is simple and satisfying. We will taste delicious appetizers with aromatic dips, the famous *mojos*, excellent soups like *potaje de berros, puchero* and *rancho* – brimming with fresh vegetables and delicate herbs, light and flavorful meat dishes and exquisite delights from the sea such as *sancocho*, which is even better on the Islands because of the extraordinarily fresh fish, recipes that are made with eggs and vegetables, and the unforgettable *papas arrugadas*. Our little tour ends with the desserts: irresistible, yet with no frills, like *bien-me-sabe*. Then on dedicated pages we will get to know more about the Islands' specialties: *papas* and *plátanos*, the healthy, nutritious and almost omnipresent *gofio*, fish, both rare and common varieties, the delicious cheeses that include two with D.o.c. designations, the fruits, the wines and the spirits.

IMPORTANT

Most of our recipes, especially the more complex ones, are presented with step-by-step photographs. We recommend that before starting you first read the list of ingredients, along with information about preparation and cooking times, level of difficulty, nutritional value and then carefully go through the instructions. These recipes all originated in metric units and conversions can be a problem. Here the quantities have been rounded up or down according to common sense and convenience. For example, 8 ounces are 225 grams, 200 grams have been converted as 8 ounces as have 250 grams, depending on the ingredients. Cooking is a question of proportions. Oven temperatures are given in both Celsius and Fahrenheit.

THE NUTRITIONIST'S ADVICE

The Canary islands are the "Fortunate Islands," not just in name, but also and mainly, because of their foods. Not only are the foods tasty, they are made with wholesome ingredients, from the grain and legumes that are the energy providers, to the wide use of greens that supply good fiber. Then there is the abundance of Atlantic and Mediterranean fish, rich in polyunsaturated fatty acids that are good for the circulation. The wide scale use of extra virgin olive oil, the fact that there is almost no butter or lard, along with one-dish meals rich in legumes, and the prevalence of white meats – kid and poultry – healthful companions to fish are all positive factors. It is a clearly Mediterranean type diet even though the Islands are located outside of the basin. The food culture is that of Mediterranean lands with the features we have mentioned. You will find several recipes with low calories and few, if any, animal fats. It is a culture that is not only praiseworthy, indeed, it should be promoted!

Fresh fish are sold in the street markets of Puerto de las Nieves on Gran Canaria. Above, "plátanos", the famous local bananas.

THE RECIPES

1: VAMOS A EMPEZAR...

Fish croquettes (Croquetas de cherne) .... page 8
Golden fish sticks (Churros de pescada) .... " 11
Oven-baked fish (Gueldes al horno).................. " 11
Potato croquettes (Albóndigas de papas) .... " 8
Potatoes and dips (Papas con mojos)............... " 14
Saucy Appetizers (Enyesques y mojos) .... " 12

The Gofio .... " 15

2: CALDOS, POTAJES Y SOPAS

Bread soup with egg
(Sopa de pan y huevos) .... page 30
Carrot Soup (Sopa de zanahorias) .... " 29
Egg and garlic soup (Sopa de huevo y ajo)........ " 26
Fish Soup (Caldo de pescado) .... " 18
Gofio Soup (Sopa de gofio) .... " 21
Meat and legume soup with pasta
(Rancho canario)... " 24
Meat and Vegetable Soup (Puchero canario).... " 23
Tenerife Fish Soup (Sopa tinerfeña).................. " 26
Tomato Soup (Sopa de tomate)......................... " 29
Watercress soup (Potaje de berros)................... " 21

3: CARNES Y AVES

Banana tenderloin
(Solomillo al plátano canario) .... page 49
Liver with savory sauce (Las Carajacas)............ " 44
Marinated kid (Cabrito al salmorejo)................. " 35
Marinated rabbit (Conejo en salmorejo)............ " 36
Meat and vegetable stew
(Ropa vieja canaria) .... " 46
Rabbit in El Hierro sauce
(Conejo en salsa herreña) .... " 40
Boiled chicken with vegetables
(Cazuela de gallina) .... " 40
Rabbit with wild fennel (Conejo al hinojo) .... " 39
Ribs with corn on the cob
(Costillas con piñas de millo) .... " 36
Roast kid (Cabrito al horno)............................. " 32
Spicy chicken stew (Pollo embarrado)............... " 44
Stewed hen (Gallina a la caitraca) .... " 42

The Fish .... " 50

4: PESCADOS

Calamari with vegetables
(Calamares a lo Nina).................................. page 57
Conger eel with wheat meal
(Congrio con escaldón) .... " 54
Dentex fritters (Albóndigas de pescado)............ " 52
Dentex with watercress (Sama con berros) .... " 68
Fish and onion stew
(Encebollado de pescado) .... " 61
Fish with potatoes and salsa (El Sancocho)....... " 66
Fish with onions (Viejas encebolladas) .... " 66
Fried Moray Eel (Morena frita) .... " 62
Marinated tuna (Atún en adobo) .... " 54
Octopus with vinegar (Pulpos canarios)............ " 64
Orange fish fillets (Mero a la naranja) .... " 62
Sardines with tomatoes (Sardinas con tomate) .. " 64
Stuffed calamari (Calamares rellenos) .... " 58

5: HUEVOS Y VERDURAS

Beans with vinegar dressing
(Judías a la vinagreta) .... page 74
Potato loaf (El Escacho) .... " 72
Salted potatoes (Papas arrugadas)..................... " 75
Stewed chickpeas (Garbanzos compuestos) ...... " 72
Stuffed tomatoes
(Tomates al estilo de Las Palmas) .... " 77
Vegetable omelets (Tortillas canarias)................ " 70

The Cheeses .... " 78

6: POSTRES

Almond terrine (Gofio de almendras) .... page 85
Milk and honey pudding (Leche asada) .... " 86
Anise loaf (Pan dulce de los Altos de Tejeda) .... " 86
Cheese dumplings (Truchas de queso) .... " 90
Coconut custard (Bien-me-sabe) .... " 80
Fried triangles (Pestiños) .... " 89
Milk rolls (Bollos de leche) .... " 82
Sweet cornbread (Frangollo) .... " 85
Sweet potato cake (Torta de batatas) .... " 89
Banana fritters (Tortitas de plátano) .... " 90
Sweet potato fritters (Buñuelos de batatas) .... " 82

Treasures of the Hesperides and Gifts of Bacchus " 92

6

Vamos a empezar...

Our tour of the gastronomic delights of the Canary Islands begins with a few tempting ideas. They are the perfect appetizers to prepare the palate for the Islands' many specialties. In addition to the myriad varieties of fish that swim in the offshore waters, we will also become acquainted with mojos, the aromatic, cold and spicy sauces that are on every table. If we want to be very precise, mojos were not created as dips for hors d'oeuvres at cocktail time – which in itself is a concept alien to the local eating habits – but rather to highlight soups and main dishes with a touch of fragrant herbs, spices and hot peppers. But, in any case they are delicious and stimulating. And there are the papas, the potatoes that make an appearance in every course... And now enough talk, the food is waiting! One more thing, the quantities in this chapter are specifically for appetizers, hors d'oeuvres or tapas – call them what you will – and let's begin!

1

ALBÓNDIGAS DE PAPAS

Potato croquettes ▶

1 Wash the potatoes. Cook in lightly salted boiling water for about 15 minutes; peel while still hot and mash them. Peel the garlic, chop together with a sprig of parsley, add this to the potatoes along with 1 slightly beaten egg. Salt to taste and blend thoroughly. Set aside for 20 minutes.

2 Break 2 eggs into a separate bowl, beat lightly with a fork. With a teaspoon take some of the potato mixture, roll a little ball with your hands. Repeat. Put the potato balls into the beaten egg and let them "sit" for 10 minutes, turning occasionally. Fry in hot oil until golden, remove and drain on paper towels. Garnish with lemon wedges and parsley. If you like you can also serve it with parsley-based *mojo verde* (see page 14).

You have just met another protagonist of Canary Island foods: the potato, or la papa, as it is called locally. Lots of varieties are grown here, each prepared in a specific way. The negra is considered the best. In addition to papas that compete with corn as the staple ingredient in the archipelago's foods, sweet potatoes, batata, also rank high (see page 82).

CROQUETAS DE CHERNE

Fish croquettes

400 gr/14 oz *cherne* fillets
  (see page 50)
1 onion
2 eggs
2 dl/ 1 cup milk
30 gr/1 oz flour
40 gr/1 oz breadcrumbs
1 1/2 lemons
  (also for garnish)
Nutmeg
Parsley
  (also for garnish)
Salt
30 gr/1 oz butter
Oil for frying
Olive oil

Servings: 6-8	
Preparation time: 35'	
Cooking time: 30'	
Difficulty: ●●	
Flavor: ●●●	
Kcal (per serving): 476	
Proteins (per serving): 17	
Fats (per serving): 38	
Nutritional value: ●●●	

Poach the *cherne* fillets (you can also use grouper or codfish) in lightly salted boiling water for about 8 minutes. Drain, pat dry and reduce to a mash in the blender. Clean the onion, chop finely and slowly wilt it in a skillet with 2 tablespoons olive oil. After 5 minutes remove from the stove and add it to the fish along with the juice of half a lemon, a sprig of finely chopped parsley, and a pinch each of salt and freshly ground nutmeg. Mix gently.
Melt the butter in a saucepan over a medium-low flame slowly add the flour, stirring constantly to avoid lumps, gradually add the lukewarm milk and a pinch of salt (keep on stirring!) until you have a creamy béchamel sauce. Let it cool to lukewarm then blend it into the fish mixture. Cool. Take a tablespoon of the mixture, shape it into an oblong croquette, dip it into the beaten egg for 2 minutes, then coat with breadcrumbs (or *gofio*, see page 15). Fry a few croquettes at a time in hot oil, remove with a slotted spoon when golden, drain on paper towels. Serve garnished with lemon wedges and sprigs of parsley.

500 gr/1 lb *papas* (medium-small potatoes)	Salt	Servings: 6-8
3 eggs	Oil for frying	Preparation time: 25'+30'
2 cloves garlic		Cooking time: 35'
Parsley (also for garnish)		Difficulty: ●●
1 lemon (for garnish)		Flavor: ●●
		Kcal (per serving): 304
		Proteins (per serving): 7
		Fats (per serving): 25
		Nutritional value: ●●●

CHURROS DE PESCADA

◄ Golden fish sticks

1 Put the fish fillets in a bowl, cover with the milk and set aside for 1 hour. In the meantime prepare the sweet and sour *mojo*. In a mortar (or the blender) combine the peeled garlic, coriander, a pinch of cumin seeds and a pinch of salt. Put the paste into a bowl, blend in the sugar, a tablespoon of vinegar, half a glass of olive oil and enough water to make a rather thin sauce. Set aside, while you prepare the *churros*.

2 In a bowl combine the flour, slightly beaten egg, 4 tablespoons olive oil, a pinch of salt and enough water to make a thick batter. Drain the fish, cut into even strips, dunk in the batter to coat thickly and fry in hot oil. Use a slotted spoon to remove them when they are golden, drain on paper towels, salt slightly and serve garnished with lemon slices and parsley, with the *mojo* as the condiment.

500 gr/1 lb codfish fillets
  (or grouper, dentex or
  other white fish)
1 egg
4dl /2 cups milk
60 gr/2 oz flour
1 lemon and parsley
  (for garnish)
Salt
Olive oil
Oil for frying

For the mojo:
2-3 cloves garlic
1 teaspoon sugar
Cumin
1 sprig fresh coriander
White wine vinegar
Coarse salt
Olive oil

Servings: 6-8	
Preparation time: 20'+1h	
Cooking time: 20'	
Difficulty: ● ●	
Flavor: ● ● ●	
Kcal (per serving): 454	
Proteins (per serving): 16	
Fats (per serving): 37	
Nutritional value: ● ● ●	

GUELDES AL HORNO

Oven-baked fish

500 gr/1 lb *gueldes*
  (see page 50)
3 cloves garlic
1 fresh, hot green pepper
1 lemon
Red wine vinegar
Salt
Olive oil

Servings: 6	
Preparation time: 20'	
Cooking time: 20'	
Difficulty: ● ●	
Flavor: ● ● ●	
Kcal (per serving): 161	
Proteins (per serving): 15	
Fats (per serving): 10	
Nutritional value: ● ●	

Preheat the oven to 200°C (400°F). Squeeze the lemon. Clean, gut, rinse and dry the *gueldes* (they should not be more than 10 cm /4 inches long). Grease the bottom of an oven-dish with a little olive oil, arrange the fish side-by-side, moisten with the lemon juice, add a little salt. Cover with aluminum foil and bake for just under 20 minutes. Heat half a glass of olive oil in a skillet, throw in the peeled, thinly sliced garlic, the chopped hot pepper, add 2 tablespoons vinegar and stir. Remove the fish from the oven, drench with the sauce. They are delicious hot or cold. If you cannot find *gueldes*, other small fish such as hake, cod, gray mullet are also suitable.

ENYESQUES Y MOJOS

Saucy Appetizers

For the mojo de queso:
70 gr/ 2 oz queso de Flor
  curado
  (see page 78)
1 head garlic
Pimentón fuerte
  (see below)
Cumin
Salt
Strips of toasted bread and
  fried gofio (see page 15)

For the mojo de tomates
  asados:
2 ripe tomatoes
1 head garlic
Coriander and cumin
  (seeds)
Salt
Vinegar
100 gr/4 oz shrimp
4-5 papas arrugadas
  (as the side dish,
  see page 75)

For the mojo picón:
2 heads garlic
4 fresh, hot red peppers
Pimentón fuerte
  (see below)
Cumin
1/4 grilled chicken breast
Salt
Vinegar

Assorted olives, crudités and
  queso tierno de San Mateo
  (see page 78)
Coarse kitchen salt
Olive oil

T o make the *mojo de queso* crush the cheese in a mortar along with the peeled garlic, a pinch each of cumin and salt (or put it through the blender) until you get a smooth paste. Blend in 1 teaspoon *pimentón*, 4 tablespoons olive oil and enough water to make a sauce thick enough for dipping strips of toasted bread, focaccia, fried *gofio* (see page 15) or fried cornmeal. This *mojo* is also a delicious condiment for vegetable soups. You can use aged Asiago or similar cheeses as a substitute.

T o make the *mojo de tomates asados*, wash the tomatoes, remove the stems. Put them under the broiler (or grill over hot coals) for 7 minutes. Peel and cut them open, remove the seeds. In a mortar (or blender) crush the peeled garlic, a dash each of cumin and salt, add the tomatoes and continue blending until you get a smooth paste. Add 6 tablespoons olive oil, 1 teaspoon vinegar and enough water to make a dip thick enough for the shrimp or *papas arrugadas* (see page 75). To prepare the shrimp: scald in slightly salted boiling water for about 8 minutes.

T o make the *mojo picón* in a mortar (or blender) combine the peeled garlic, the hot peppers – make sure you remove the seeds, and a dash each of cumin and salt. Add a level tablespoon of *pimentón*, a glass of olive oil, drop-by-drop blend in 2 tablespoons vinegar, stirring gently to make sauce thick enough for strips of grilled chicken (or steamed fish).
Serve the *mojos* with their respective "accompaniments" at cocktail time, along with different types of green and black olives, and crudités (raw carrots, celery, bell peppers, zucchini, etc.) cut into strips, and with *queso tierno* (see page 78) the soft, fresh cheese from the Islands. You can also use *crescenza, sahnequark* or similar varieties. Refrigerate the *mojos* in well-closed containers.

Servings: 8	
Preparation time: 35'	
Cooking time: 10'	
Difficulty: ●●	
Flavor: ●●●	
Kcal (per serving): 131	
Proteins (per serving): 11	
Fats (per serving): 10	
Nutritional value: ●●	

Mojos are the pride and symbol of the archipelago, you can find them on every table throughout the Islands. In addition to being served with every course – except perhaps dessert, and that is only a "perhaps" – they are a delightful prelude to any meal, or a fine excuse to enjoy a glass of local wine with friends. Pimentón is a condiment, that need not be very hot, and is common throughout the Iberian lands. It is made from dried, ground peppers, of the genus capsicum annuum, that are as intensely red as they are flavorful. In Spain there are both the *fuerte* and *dulce* varieties – the choice is a matter of personal taste. It is an ingredient essential to the outcome of the recipe, not a mere a touch to enliven a dish. In English speaking countries it is commonly translated as paprika, but it is not at all Hungarian paprika that is obtained from more pungent peppers originally grown in India. Pimentón is made with species from Africa and the New World. Although it is different in flavor and final results, you can indeed use sweet or hot paprika, or even the chili powders found in organic food shops in lieu of pimentón.

PAPAS CON MOJOS

Potatoes and dips

600 gr/1 lb *papas*   (medium-small potatoes)

For the mojo colorado:
- 2-3 cloves garlic
- 1 fresh red chili pepper
- *Pimentón dulce*
  (see page 12)
- Cumin
- Fresh oregano, 1 sprig
- Vinegar
- Salt
- Olive oil

For the mojo verde:
- 4 cloves garlic
- 1 fresh red chili pepper
- Parsley (a nice bunch, finely
  chopped)
- Coriander seeds
- Cumin
- Fresh oregano, 1 sprig
- Vinegar
- Salt
- Olive oil

Servings: 6-8	
Preparation time: 20'	
Cooking time: 10'	
Difficulty: ●	
Flavor: ● ●	
Kcal (per serving): 274	
Proteins (per serving): 1	
Fats (per serving): 25	
Nutritional value: ● ●	

Wash the potatoes, cook them in their jackets in lightly salted water until they just soft enough to cut. Peel and slice into rounds. Arrange on a platter, and serve with the dips.

1 In a mortar (or blender) reduce the peeled garlic and chili pepper to a paste. Transfer to a bowl. Then, by hand blend in 1 teaspoon *pimentón*, half a teaspoon cumin, the oregano leaves, 3-4 tablespoons olive oil, 3 tablespoons vinegar, salt, and enough water to make a sauce that is just thick enough for dipping.

2 In a mortar (or blender) reduce the peeled garlic, chili pepper and 1 teaspoon coriander seeds to a paste. Transfer to a bowl, then by hand, blend in the parsley, a pinch of cumin, the oregano leaves, 3 tablespoons olive oil, 3 tablespoons vinegar, salt, and enough water to make a sauce that is thick enough for dipping. Serve the two dips side by side.

THE GOFIO

Gofio is by far the most popular traditional food on the Islands. It complements any course, from soup to dessert when it is not the main dish. It is also the

symbol of the archipelago's foods and ranks second only to plâtano the bananas that have made the Canary Islands famous throughout the world.

It is not an exaggeration to say that gofio is part of the islanders' metabolism. Not only have they been making and using it day in and day out for millennia, combined with water, broth, oil or other foods, heedless of changing eating habits and fashions (brought about in part by the hordes of tourists who flock to the Islands season after season), demand is actually rising – even from abroad. From a traditional, primitive food, because of its versatility in the kitchen and on the table as well as its compatibility with any diet, and by virtue of its nutritional values, gofio has been elevated to the rank of dietetic product.

Gofio is a meal made from grains – mainly wheat, corn and barley – that are toasted and milled singly or together. Some legumes are blended in: chickpeas or flat peas or fava beans – in the north of the island of Hierro – which add a touch of distinctive flavor and make it creamy. The most popular varieties are gofio de millo (made of corn), gofio de trigo (wheat) and de cebada (barley). Another widely used version is gofio de mezcla, also known as tres cereals con garbanzos that combines corn, wheat and barley with chickpeas. Not only does each of the seven islands have its favorite, but each village and even family has its own distinctive tastes that are hard to eliminate. Today gofio can be found on the Spanish mainland and in other European countries, in shops specializing in organic or dietetic foods. Its quality is so special that it is hard to replace, except with fine meals of well toasted cereals. For example, instead of gofio de millo you can use cornmeal toasted in a hot skillet with no fat or grease, but once you have tasted the genuine gofio you will quickly notice the difference.

The History and How

Who invented gofio? Asking this question is rather like trying to discover who invented broth, polenta or omelets; its origins have been lost in time. As old as the Canary Islands themselves, gofio was the staple food of the natives even before the Phoenicians or other navigators set foot on the Islands. Originally, due to the scarce or inexistent trade in seeds it seems that it was made solely from barley. Later they added wheat, oats and fava beans. In times of famine they were replaced by wild Gramineae – about a dozen varieties – that experience and necessity made into custom. Next came rye (centeno), chickpeas and finally millo, that is corn.

For the first phase in preparing gofio, that is toasting, the people used a large terracotta dish known as the tiesto or tostadora, that varied from 50 to 100 centimeters (maximum 3 feet) in diameter that was set on the fire on three stones called chíniques or tíniques. Some people still use the tiesto today. Even though the traditional method is time consuming and costly it does guarantee the best quality. A layer of black, volcanic sand is spread in the tostadora, and then the cereals or legumes are put on top to be toasted over a fire, stirred with a wooden or cane implement called the juercán with the handle wrapped in rags. The toasted kernels are sifted to eliminate sand and impurities, sometimes salt or sugar are added to make tafeña.

For centuries the most delicate phase, grinding, was done by molinos, simple but brilliant devices comprising two muelas, round, convex stones carved into the piedra molinera consisting of more or less fine grain basalt, one on top of the other so that the two flat sides faced each other. The toasted kernels were poured in through a hole in the middle of the upper muela. One or more muescas, small cavities on the edge made it possible to turn it using hands, animal bones, wooden sticks or cane. The lower muela also had an opening for inserting a pin planted into the ground that would keep it horizontal. The slow manual grinding guaranteed – and still does so today – a product with exceptional aroma, flavor and consistency. Even today, it is the only one that can satisfy the demanding tastes of the Canary Islanders in spite of the fact that it is much more expensive the common gofio. And they are demanding tastes indeed: the coarser meal obtained at the beginning and end of the milling process known as rolón or afrecho is usually considered animal feed. Even today, there are people who make gofio the way their ancestors did for generations. In some villages, such as Chipude on the Island of La Gomera and Los Mocanes on Hierro they still use stone molinos, in other places you can still see systems with four or more muescas, so that several pairs of hands can work at once.

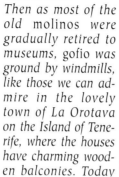

Then as most of the old molinos were gradually retired to museums, gofio was ground by windmills, like those we can admire in the lovely town of La Orotava on the Island of Tenerife, where the houses have charming wooden balconies. Today gofio is made in modern plants with industrial toasting systems and electric mills.

In the kitchen, on the table

For thousands of years gofio has been the "daily bread" of the Canary Islands. After having fed the primitive peoples, it sustained the humble for generations, mixed with hot water or broth, or oil, honey, cheese or whatever was available. Today, in less lean times, taste and imagination bring us gofio in different and appetizing, sweet or savory forms. But it was not always so. Gofio was a subsistence food, a staple and people said prayers of thanks when they had sufficient supplies. Since fine cereals, such as wheat, corn and barely, were rare, they would grind wild plants such as cosco, a creeper with tiny red leaves that grows along the coasts, barrilla or vidrio to make an edible coarse meal. Often they used lupin (chochos) that yields a coarser meal, but in times of need, anything is grist for the mill.

Gofio, as we have been saying, is so much a part of the local diet that it is almost synonymous with food itself. Gofión , meaning glutton, was how the chicharreros, the natives of Tenerife, described the inhabitants of Gran Canaria. And on the subject of vocabulary, in addition to the ancient tools, tradition has conserved a rich lexicon concerning the various phases of making, using and eating gofio. Regarding the mixtures of gofio and various liquids and other ingredients, the locals distinguish gofio revuelto mixed with hot water from escaldón and rala, mixed with hot broth or diluted in broth, milk or wine, not to mention berrendo, blended with water and bits of cheese. And then, if it is prepared with not enough liquid it becomes gofio jaragán a chalky, inedible paste instead of the smooth blend it should be. Woe to the kitchen where you hear the words "Este gofio quedó jaragán!" It means that the whole mass has to be thrown out and started over. There is even a specific glossary for eating gofio. Cabrillas are plain, "powdery" gofio eaten by the spoonful with a good glass of wine; a handful shaped with the fingers is called gainás, gasnais or goga. And then, if you want to bring it to the table, it is important to know that a pan de gofio is much smaller than a billarda – or bimba or brimba – de gofio, while a pella is an oblong or round portion, like the type served with sancocho (see page 66).

The fortunes of gofio

Emigrants who set out from the Canary Islands always took a sack of gofio along. It was a food that met with great success in the New World, especially Venezuela, Uruguay, Brazil and Argentina, where frangollo (see page 85) is also very popular. And who knows, perhaps Christopher Columbus included this magical meal in his supplies when he docked at the Canary Islands on his way to America. Today no one eats gofio out of need, but rather to delight the palate and for health. It is rich in B vitamins, proteins, fiber, vitamin C and minerals (calcium, iron, manganese and others). Of the many varieties available on the market, gofio de mezcla made of at least three fine cereals and chickpeas is the richest in calories, proteins and carbohydrates. Of the single-grain types, barley gofio is the lowest in fats, while corn gofio has the most of all. Then, if corn gofio is the richest in fiber, the variety made from barley has the most soluble fiber, while wheat gofio has the highest mineral content.

Thanks to its dietetic and nutritional properties, gofio that contains no food colorings or preservatives, is without a doubt a real health-food. Like many other "poor" foods it is suitable – according to type – for special diets and needs, such as those of infants. People who are not accustomed to it from birth may find it a little tasteless, so at the start it is best to try it blended with broth or honey – if you like it sweet – rather than with plain water and gradually develop a taste for its delicate flavor.

CALDOS, POTAJES Y SOPAS

This section brings us some of the most popular foods from the Canary Islands. They are the recipes that for generations nourished fishermen, shepherds and farmers. Often these three occupations met – and still do so today – in one person so that soups use ocean fish, products of the fields and pastures. More often than not rather than "first-courses" they are tributes to old customs that did not divide meals into several courses. Here are true one-dish meals And when you taste puchero or rancho you will be enjoying a full meal – with broth and greens and legumes, farm-raised meat, fresh fish, as well as the cheese which, though not listed among the ingredients – is always served separately – to be enjoyed between one spoonful and the next.

2

CALDO DE PESCADO

Fish Soup

1 Put the garlic under the broiler until it is dark and wrinkled. Set aside. Clean all the vegetables, remembering to peel the potatoes and remove the seeds from the tomatoes, chili pepper and bell pepper.

2 Quickly sauté the fish fillets in a skillet with 3 tablespoons olive oil (2 minutes on each side). Remove with a slotted spoon, drain on paper towels and keep warm.

3 Finely chop the onion, and sauté it in 5 tablespoons olive oil in a terracotta soup pot. When it is transparent add the cut-up tomatoes, the bell pepper cut into strips, the peeled garlic, chili pepper and *bouquet garni*.

4 Cook slowly for about ten minutes, then add the potatoes – cut into chunks if necessary – and the fish fillets. In the meantime heat 2.5 liters (2.5 quarts) water, dissolve the saffron and a pinch of salt. Add it to the pot, cover and simmer for about 10 minutes, or until the potatoes are *al dente*. Remove the *bouquet* pour the broth with the vegetables and fish into a soup tureen, let stand for 10-15 minutes and then served garnished with parsley sprigs.

700 gr/ 1 ½ lbs assorted
  fish fillets (*sama, cherne, mero*, etc. see page 50)
10 *papas*
  (medium-small potatoes)
2 tomatoes
1 bell pepper
1 onion
1 head garlic
1 fresh chili pepper
1 *bouquet garni*
  (1 bay leaf, coriander leaves and thyme)
Saffron
  (one sachet)
Parsley
  (for garnish)
Salt
Olive oil

Servings: 6	
Preparation time: 20'+15'	
Cooking time: 45'	
Difficulty: ●●●	
Flavor: ●●●	
Kcal (per serving): 331	
Proteins (per serving): 24	
Fats (per serving): 11	
Nutritional value: ●	

POTAJE DE BERROS

◀ Watercress soup

250 gr/8 oz watercress (one bunch)
300 gr/12 oz salted pork ribs
200 gr/8 oz dried white beans
4-5 *papas* (medium-small potatoes)
1 cob corn
1 onion
4 cloves garlic
60 gr/2 oz *gofio de millo* (see page 15)
Salt
Olive oil

Servings:	6
Preparation time:	20'+5h
Cooking time:	1h + 15'
Difficulty:	●●
Flavor:	●●
Kcal (per serving):	405
Proteins (per serving):	18
Fats (per serving):	13
Nutritional value:	●

S oak the beans in cold water for 5 hours before you start. Put the ribs in lukewarm water and leave them there until you need them (if you cannot get salted ribs, use fresh ones, but you will have to add a little more salt when cooking to compensate). Clean the greens, including the watercress; remember to peel the potatoes and shell the corn. Drain the beans and put them into a large pot with the ribs. Finely chop the watercress, add it to the pot along with the coarsely cut onion, and finely sliced garlic. Add 4 tablespoons olive oil, cover with water (about 2.5 liters/2.5 quarts) and add a pinch of salt. Slowly bring to the boil, cover and simmer for 30 minutes. Add the corn kernels and cubed potatoes, cover and cook slowly for another 30 minutes. When it is ready, let the *potaje* set covered for 15 minutes, sprinkle with *gofio* and serve.

Used in many traditional Island recipes, berro *(or plural* berros) *is one of the glories of the archipelago.* *In some parts of Spain it is called* mastuerzo acuático *(lat.* nasturtium officinale)*, we know it as* watercress, *the Germans call it* Brunnenkresse, *the Italians* crescione *and in French it is* cresson de fontaine.

SOPA DE GOFIO

Gofio Soup

1.5 liters/ 1.5 quarts fish broth (see page 18)
1 onion
60 gr/ 2 oz *gofio de millo* (see page 15)
Mojo verde (see page 14)
Salt
Olive oil

Servings:	4
Preparation time:	10'
Cooking time:	15'
Difficulty:	●
Flavor:	●●●
Kcal (per serving):	272
Proteins (per serving):	6
Fats (per serving):	21
Nutritional value:	●

U sing fish broth or the saffron flavored *caldo de pescado* (see page 18) setting the fish aside for the main course, you can make this simple and delicious soup. If you cannot find *gofio* you can use cornmeal, toasted in a hot skillet without any fats or grease – and dress it with fragrant *mojo verde*. Clean the onion, chop it finely and sauté it gently in a large pot with 4 tablespoons olive oil. After 5 minutes add the *gofio*, stir and brown it over a medium flame. Pour in the hot broth, stirring constantly, salt to taste and bring to the boil. Lower the flame, cook until thick. Serve the soup in with a small bowl of *mojo verde* so that each guest can help himself.

PUCHERO CANARIO

Meat and Vegetable Soup

250 gr/8 oz dried white
   beans
500 gr/1 lb boned loin
   of pork
150 gr/6 oz bacon
1 onion
3 cloves garlic
2 *papas* (medium potatoes)
2 cobs of corn
1 bunch beet greens
2 ripe tomatoes
1 zucchini
150 gr/6 oz watercress
   (one bunch)
Gofio de millo
   (see page 15)
Coriander leaves
   (also for garnish)
Parsley (also for garnish)
Salt and pepper
Olive oil

Servings: 4	
Preparation time: 25'+ 5h	
Cooking time: 1h 30'	
Difficulty: ● ● ●	
Flavor: ● ●	
Kcal (per serving): 1027	
Proteins (per serving): 44	
Fats (per serving): 59	
Nutritional value: ● ● ●	

1 As usual, soak the beans for 5 hours before you start. In the meantime, wash the zucchino and cut up the greens. Then, put the beans into a large pot together with the pork and bacon, cover with cold water and bring to the boil. Lower the flame and simmer for 30 minutes. Add the beet greens, watercress and zucchini, add salt and pepper to taste.

2 Peel and cube the potatoes; wash the corn cobs, remove the kernels and add them to the soup along with the potatoes. Cover and simmer until cooked (about 30 minutes). Drain the meats, arrange them on a serving platter with the greens and keep warm. Strain the broth.

3 Clean and chop the onion, slowly sauté it in a saucepan (terracotta is best) with 3-4 tablespoons olive oil, add the garlic and the tomatoes cut into chunks. Cook slowly until the tomatoes are a pulp.

4 Blend in 3-4 tablespoons *gofio* and pour on the strained broth, cook for 5-6 minutes or until the liquid boils. Serve the soup garnished with coriander and parsley. The meats and vegetables will be your delicious main course.

RANCHO CANARIO

Meat and legume soup with pasta

1 Soak the chickpeas in water for 6 hours before you start. Prepare the vegetables, remember to remove the seeds from the tomatoes, and peel and cube the potatoes. Finely chop the onion and sauté it gently with 4 tablespoons olive oil in a large terracotta pot. After 5 minutes add the chopped tomatoes.

2 Cook and stir for 8 minutes, then add the meat along with crumbled *chorizo*, brown over a low flame for 6 minutes.

3 Add the chickpeas and potatoes, one tablespoon *pimentón*, a pinch of salt, the saffron and enough water to cover it all. Cover the pot and bring to the boil. Simmer for one hour, by then the potatoes will have softened entirely, making the soup thick.

4 Uncover the pot and add the *fideos*. Bring to the boil and then turn off the flame immediately and remove the pot from the stove. Cover and let the *rancho* set for 30 minutes. Serve lukewarm. Even though we have included it among the soups, it is obviously a hearty, one-dish meal.

Chorizo is the most popular of Iberian sausages made of chopped lean and fatty pork (sometimes there is beef as well), generously flavored with ground chili pepper, garlic, pepper and other spices. It is quite similar to Southern Italian spicy sausage. There are several varieties on the market, distinguished by different color labels. For tapas and bocadillos we recommend the aged variety (3 months old), whereas the fresh type is best for cooking.

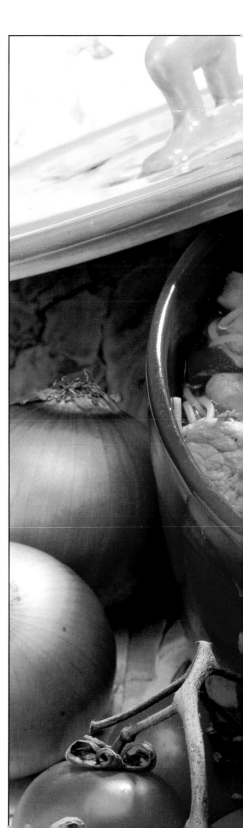

250 gr/8 oz *fideos* (fidelini or thin spaghetti)	4 *papas* (medium potatoes)	**Servings:** 4
	2 ripe tomatoes	**Preparation time:** 15'+6h
250 gr/8 oz Dried chickpeas	1 onion	**Cooking time:** 1h 20'+30'
500 gr/1 lb boned loin of pork, cut into bite-size pieces	*Pimentón dulce* (see page 12)	**Difficulty:** ●●
		Flavor: ●●●
	Saffron (one sachet)	**Kcal (per serving):** 940
150 gr/6 oz *chorizo* (see opposite page)	Salt	**Proteins (per serving):** 59
	Olive oil	**Fats (per serving):** 32
		Nutritional value: ●●●

3

4

SOPA TINERFEÑA

Tenerife Fish Soup ▶

500 gr/1 lb fish
(*soma, cherne, mero*, etc.,
see page 50)
2 dozen *papas*
(small potatoes)
3 tomatoes
Cumin
Saffron (1 sachet)
Coriander leaves
(for garnish)
4 slices toasted
country bread
Salt

Servings: 4	
Preparation time: 15'	
Cooking time: 25'	
Difficulty: ●	
Flavor: ● ● ●	
Kcal (per serving): 307	
Proteins (per serving): 29	
Fats (per serving): 2	
Nutritional value: ●	

W ash the tomatoes, cut them into quarters and remove the seeds; peel the potatoes but leave them whole.
Put the tomatoes and potatoes into a pot with a pinch each of salt and cumin, add a little less than 2 liters/ 2 quarts water. Bring to the boil and simmer for about 20 minutes. Add the fish fillets and saffron, cook until the fish is done and tender. Remove the fish with a slotted spoon and arrange in individual soup bowls on top of a slice of toasted bread. Add the potatoes and broth, garnish with coriander sprigs and serve. This is a one dish meal, simple to make, delicious to eat and has no added fats.

SOPA DE HUEVO Y AJO

Egg and garlic soup

200 gr/8 oz *fideos*
(fidelini or thin spaghetti)
1 head garlic
2 ripe tomatoes
4 egg yolks
Coriander leaves
(for garnish)
160 gr /6 oz *queso de Flor curado* in flakes
(see page 78)
Salt
Olive oil

Servings: 4	
Preparation time: 10'	
Cooking time: 30'	
Difficulty: ● ●	
Flavor: ● ● ●	
Kcal (per serving): 581	
Proteins (per serving): 29	
Fats (per serving): 32	
Nutritional value: ● ●	

W ash the tomatoes, cut into chunks and remove the seeds. Peel the garlic, slowly sauté it in a soup pot with 4 tablespoons olive oil, after 3 minutes add the tomatoes. Stir and cook for 5 minutes, add 1 liter/1 quart hot water, salt to taste, cover and bring to a gentle boil for 15 minutes. Add the *fideos*, and continue cooking until the pasta is *al dente*. Ladle out the soup into individual bowls, put an egg yolk in each bowl – be careful not to break them – and sprinkle with flaked *queso Flor* (you can also use any well-aged cheese made from ewe's or cow's milk), garnish with coriander and serve.

SOPA DE TOMATE

Tomato Soup

1 kg/2 lbs ripe tomatoes
2 bell peppers
1 onion
2 cloves garlic
Sugar
Pimentón dulce (see page 12)
Oregano (for garnish)
Salt
Olive oil

Servings:	6
Preparation time:	8'
Cooking time:	18'
Difficulty:	●●
Flavor:	●●●
Kcal (per serving):	201
Proteins (per serving):	41
Fats (per serving):	2
Nutritional value:	●

C lean the vegetables, and remember to remove the seeds. Finely chop the onion with the garlic, and sauté in a soup pot (preferably terracotta) with 4-5 tablespoons olive oil. When it is transparent add the cut-up vegetables; cook for 5 minutes then add 1 tablespoon sugar, 1 teaspoon *pimentón* and a pinch of salt. Cover with hot water (a little over 1 liter/1 quart), bring to the boil, cover the pot and boil over a medium flame for about 10 minutes. Serve the soup with a sprig of oregano in each bowl as garnish.

SOPA DE ZANAHORIAS

Carrot Soup

600 gr/1 ¼ lbs medium carrots
1 onion
160 gr/ 6 oz *queso de Flor curado* in flakes (see page 78)
60 gr/ 2 oz *gofio de millo* (see page 15)
Sugar
Parsley (for garnish)
White wine vinegar
Salt
10 g/1 pat Lard
Olive oil

Servings:	4
Preparation time:	20'
Cooking time:	35'
Difficulty:	●●
Flavor:	●●
Kcal (per serving):	387
Proteins (per serving):	15
Fats (per serving):	24
Nutritional value:	●

C lean the carrots, cook them in lightly salted boiling water (about 2 liters/2 quarts) for about 20 minutes. Drain the carrots (strain the cooking liquid and set it aside) and cut them into circles. Clean and slice the onion, gently wilt it in a soup pot (use terracotta if you can) with 3 tablespoons olive oil and the melted cooking fat. After 5 minutes add the carrots. Add 2 tablespoons vinegar, raise the flame so that it evaporates quickly, then stir in 1 teaspoon sugar and the *gofio*. Lower the flame, add the liquid from the carrots (reduced to 1 liter/1 quart), boil for 5 minutes, salt to taste. Serve with a sprinkling of flaked *queso Flor,* (or other aged cheese made from ewe's or cow's milk) and parsley.

SOPA DE PAN Y HUEVOS

Bread soup with egg

3 eggs
1 onion
1 liter/1 quart vegetable
  (or chicken) broth,
  ready-made
8 slices toasted country
  bread
Parsley (also for garnish)
Salt
10 gr/1 pat lard
olive oil

Servings: 4	
Preparation time: 20'	
Cooking time: 35'	
Difficulty: ● ●	
Flavor: ● ●	
Kcal (per serving): 267	
Proteins (per serving): 11	
Fats (per serving): 23	
Nutritional value: ●	

Clean the onion, chop it finely with a sprig of parsley and wilt in a pot with 4 tablespoons olive oil. After 5 minutes add the broth, salt to taste, cover and boil for 15 minutes. In the meantime, toast the bread in the oven (then leave the oven on, set to 200°C/400°F). Grease an oven dish with the lard (or butter), place the toasted bread on top; beat the eggs with 5 tablespoons boiling broth and pour over the bread, add the rest of the broth with the onion and parsley. Take care that it does not overflow. Bake for 10 minutes, decorate with sprigs of parsley and serve.

CARNES
Y AVES

Given the nature of the archipelago the preferred,
and most readily available meats, we find served in
the Canary Islands are kid, lamb and rabbit –
wrapped in the unique fragrance of the herbs that
perfume the air – followed by domestic poultry.
Hogs, too, when the meat is not made into exquisite
hams or tasty sausages, play an important role.
Although there are fewer recipes for beef and veal,
they are tasty and very original.

3

CABRITO AL HORNO

Roast kid

1 Prepare the mojo: peel the garlic and crush it in the mortar (or blender) together with the hot peppers minus the seeds, 1 tablespoon *pimentón*, 1 bay leaf and the leaves from a sprig of thyme. Transfer the paste to a bowl and blend in 1 ½ glasses wine, 6 table-spoons olive oil and a sprig of chopped parsley. Set aside until ready to use. Pre-heat the oven to 200°C/400°F.

2 Clean the half onion and slice it thinly; slice the half tomato, removing the seeds; slice the half lemon. Place the meat on your work table, use a sharp knife to make little incisions that you will fill with the onion, tomato and lemon slices.

3 Salt the meat, put it in an oven dish, moisten with 3 tablespoons *mojo* and roast for about 1 hour. Every now and then baste with the *mojo* – you will use it all, and halfway through the cooking time, turn the meat so that it browns evenly.

4 While the meat is roasting, peel the potatoes, salt and quick fry (3 minutes) in a skillet with a squiggle of oil. Drain and put them in the oven around the meat about 20 minutes before roasting time is up. Serve garnished with sprigs of parsley.

1 kg/2 lbs leg of kid	Salt	3 dl/ 1 ½ cups	**Servings:** 4
20 *papas*	Olive oil	Dry white wine	**Preparation time:** 25'
(medium-small		*Pimentón dulce*	**Cooking time:** 1h
potatoes)	*For the* mojo:	(see page 12)	**Difficulty:** ●●
½ ripe tomato	2 Heads garlic	Olive oil	**Flavor:** ●●●
½ onion	2 Fresh, hot red		**Kcal (per serving):** 629
½ lemon	peppers		**Proteins (per serving):** 43
Parsley	Bay leaves, parsley		**Fats (per serving):** 28
(for garnish)	and thyme		**Nutritional value:** ●●

CABRITO AL SALMOREJO

Marinated kid

1 Soak the *ñoras* in lukewarm water for 30 minutes before you begin. Squeeze out the excess moisture, remove the seeds and crush in the mortar (or put through the blender) together with the peeled garlic, oregano and thyme leaves, ½ teaspoon *pimentón*, salt and pepper. Transfer the paste to a bowl and dilute with 3 tablespoons vinegar.

2 Rub the shoulder all over with the diluted paste. Put in a dish, cover and let it marinate in a cool place for at least 8 hours. Drain, scrape, and save the marinade (both the liquid and the paste).

3 Cut the meat into bite-sized pieces, brown in a terracotta pan with 5 tablespoons olive oil. Cover, lower the flame and cook very slowly for at least 30 minutes until tender (add a tablespoon or two of hot water if it tends to dry while cooking). Put the meat on a serving platter and keep warm.

4 Pour all the *salmorejo*, that is the marinade (liquid and solid parts) into the oil left in the pan, cook over a lively flame for 5 minutes, then dress the meat with the sauce and serve with *papas arrugadas*. How many? About 5 or 6 per person.

Ñoras are dried peppers with a flavor that is "warm" rather than "hot." They are shaped like small lanterns and are usually dark red, almost purple.
You can use a couple of teaspoons of ground sweet paprika in their place.

A vacation village in the desert of Maspalomas.

800 gr/ 1 ¾ lbs boned
 saddle or shoulder of kid
2 *ñoras* (see above)
1 clove garlic
Pimentón fuerte
 (see page 12)
Oregano and thyme
Papas arrugadas
 (as the side dish,
 see page 75)
Vinegar
Salt and pepper
Olive oil

Servings:	4
Preparation time:	20'+8h30'
Cooking time:	40'
Difficulty:	●●
Flavor:	●●●
Kcal (per serving):	339
Proteins (per serving):	39
Fats (per serving):	18
Nutritional value:	●

COSTILLAS CON PIÑAS DE MILLO

Ribs with corn on the cob ▶

1 kg/2 lbs salted
  pork ribs
8-10 small corncobs
Parsley for garnish

Servings: 4

Preparation time: 20'+4h

Cooking time: 40'

Difficulty: ●

Flavor: ●●●

Kcal (per serving): 424

Proteins (per serving): 48

Fats (per serving): 19

Nutritional value: ●●

About 4 hours before you begin, put the ribs into lukewarm water to soak. Naturally, you can skip this step if you use unsalted ribs! Clean the corn. Put the ribs into a pot with the corncobs and cover with hot water. Add a pinch of salt only if you are using unsalted ribs. Bring to the boil, cover simmer for about 30 minutes, until the ribs are tender. Drain the meat and corn and arrange on a serving platter. Separate the ribs and cut the corncobs into circles. Sprinkle with finely chopped parsley and serve.

1 Rabbit (about 1.2 kg/
  2 ½ lbs), ready-to-cook
2 large heads of garlic
Pimentón dulce
  (see page 12)
Cumin
Dry white wine
White wine vinegar
Papas arrugadas (as the
  side dish, see page 75)
Salt
Black peppercorns
Olive oil

Servings: 4

Preparation time: 20'+8h

Cooking time: 15'

Difficulty: ●

Flavor: ●●●

Kcal (per serving): 424

Proteins (per serving): 48

Fats (per serving): 19

Nutritional value: ●●

CONEJO EN SALMOREJO

Marinated rabbit

Peel the garlic and crush it in a mortar (or put it through the blender) with 6 peppercorns, 1 teaspoon salt, and ½ teaspoon cumin to make a paste. Transfer the paste to a large bowl and blend in 12 tablespoons olive oil, 3 tablespoons vinegar, 2 tablespoons *pimentón*, and 1 glass wine. Rinse the rabbit, pat dry and cut it into twelve pieces (throw away the head). Put the pieces into the bowl with the *salmorejo*, cover and marinate in a cool place for 8 hours, turning every now and then. Cook the rabbit over a hot charcoal grill for 10-12 minutes, turning the pieces every 3 minutes and brushing with the marinade. Serve this typical local dish with *papas arrugadas*.

CONEJO AL HINOJO

Rabbit with wild fennel

1 rabbit
  (about 1.2 kgs/1 ½ lbs),
  ready-to-cook
1 onion
4 cloves garlic
1 bell pepper
2-3 ripe tomatoes
Wild fennel
  (one bunch)
Bay leaf
Pimentón fuerte
  (see page 12)
Dry white wine
Salt
Olive oil

Servings: 4	
Preparation time: 20'	
Cooking time: 1h	
Difficulty: ●●	
Flavor: ●●●	
Kcal (per serving): 434	
Proteins (per serving): 46	
Fats (per serving): 18	
Nutritional value: ●●	

1 Rinse the rabbit, pat it dry and cut it into 10-12 pieces (eliminating the head). Wash the pepper and tomatoes, remove the seeds and cut into pieces. Clean and coarsely chop the onion. In a large pot, wilt the onion with 5-6 tablespoons olive oil, then add the tomatoes and pepper, simmer for 10 minutes and then add the peeled garlic cloves.

2 When the garlic starts to brown add the rabbit, 1 bay leaf and 1 teaspoon *pimentón*. Brown the rabbit over a lively flame, turning the pieces so they cook evenly.

3 Pour 1 glass white wine over the rabbit and let it evaporate, salt to taste and add some of the fennel (tops, not the stems).

4 Add enough hot water to cover the rabbit, cover the pot and bring to the boil. Skim off the liquid, lower the flame and simmer for about 40 minutes. During the last 5-6 minutes uncover the pot to reduce the sauce, and check the salt. Serve covered with the sauce.

The charming gazebo of the Parco San Telmo in Las Palmas.

CONEJO EN SALSA HERREÑA

Rabbit in El Hierro sauce ▶

About 30 minutes before you begin, soak the bread in a little cold water. Rinse the rabbit, pat it dry and cut it into 10-12 pieces (eliminate the head). Brown the pieces in a little oil until they are evenly golden, salt lightly and keep warm. Peel the garlic, in a mortar (or blender) crush it with the squeezed out bread, 1 tablespoon *pimentón* and 1 bay leaf. Transfer the paste to a bowl, blend in 1 glass wine and 6 tablespoons olive oil, then add the leaves from one sprig each of thyme and oregano. Add enough water to make a smooth sauce that is not runny. Put the browned rabbit into a terracotta pot, pour the sauce over it and bring to the boil. Cover the pot and simmer for 40 minutes; during the last 10 minutes of cooking time remove the lid to reduce the sauce. Check the salt. Serve the rabbit garnished with bay leaves, oregano and thyme.

---

1 hen, 1.5 kg/ 3 lbs, ready-to-cook
350 gr/13 oz chickpeas
12 new potatoes
2 ripe tomatoes
1 onion
Saffron stigmas
Salt, black peppercorns
20 gr/ 1 oz lard

Servings:	6
Preparation time:	15'+4h
Cooking time:	2h20'+15'
Difficulty:	●
Flavor:	●●
Kcal (per serving):	804
Proteins (per serving):	53
Fats (per serving):	44
Nutritional value:	●●●

CAZUELA DE GALLINA

Boiled chicken with vegetables

Soak the chickpeas in cold water for 4 hours before you begin. Put the hen into a pot with the drained chickpeas (traditionally they were wrapped in a fine cloth mesh), 4 pepper corns and lots of cold water. Cover and slowly bring to the boil over a low flame. In the meantime, finely chop the onion; clean and chop the tomatoes. Wilt the onion in a skillet with the melted lard, add the tomatoes and cook slowly for 10 minutes. Add the contents of the skillet to the pot – that should be boiling – cover and simmer for about 2 hours. About 20 minutes before the cooking time is up, add the potatoes and a few saffron stigmas. When it is done, salt to taste and let the covered *cazuela* sit for 15 minutes. Cut the hen into eighths or quarters and serve with the chickpeas and potatoes. You can use the broth to make soup or other dishes.

1 rabbit (with liver), about 1.2 kg /2 ½ lbs, ready-to-cook	*Pimentón fuerte* (see page 12)	**Servings:** 4
	Red wine (see caption)	**Preparation time:** 20'+30'
2 slices day-old country bread, without the crust	Salt	**Cooking time:** 50'
	Olive oil	**Difficulty:** ● ●
1 head garlic		**Flavor:** ● ● ●
Bay leaves, oregano and thyme (also for garnish)		**Kcal (per serving):** 533
		Proteins (per serving): 52
		Fats (per serving): 19
		Nutritional value: ● ●

With this typical dish from the island of El Hierro we recommend the strong, local wine Parreño. or any other red wine as long as it is robust and full-bodied.

GALLINA A LA CAITRACA

Stewed Hen

1 The chicken should be pot-ready. Pour the broth into a pot and bring it to the boil, add the chicken. Turn it so that it cooks evenly. After 20 minutes, remove it, set it aside and keep the broth hot.

2 Put the chicken into a large, deep stewpot or Dutch oven (terracotta would be best), and brown it in the melted lard for about 10 minutes, turning it so that it is a nice, even color.

3 Add 2 glasses of wine, the peeled garlic, breadcrumbs, a sprig of parsley, 2 bay leaves, the cinnamon and about 10 pepper corns to the pot. Salt to taste, cover and slowly bring to the boil. Simmer for one and a half hours (adding a little strained broth if necessary). Remove the chicken from the pot, cut into 12 pieces, arrange them o a serving platter and keep warm.

4 Add 3 ladles of the broth to the cooking juices, cook over a low flame, blending to reduce the sauce by half. Use the sauce to dress the chicken and garnish with parsley and bay leaves. If you do not have the hearty *puchero* broth, vegetable broth will be fine, and you can substitute a crumbled zwieback for the breadcrumbs.

1 hen, 1.5 kg/3 lbs (ready-to-cook)	40 gr / 1 ½ oz Breadcrumbs	**Servings:** 6
1 liter/1 quart strained *puchero* broth (see page 23)	Dry white wine Salt and black peppercorns	**Preparation time:** 10'
		Cooking time: 2h15'
1 head garlic	60 gr /2 oz lard	**Difficulty:** ●
Parsley and bay leaves (also for garnish)		**Flavor:** ● ●
		Kcal (per serving): 730
Cinnamon, 1 stick		**Proteins (per serving):** 41
		Fats (per serving): 51
		Nutritional value: ● ● ●

POLLO EMBARRADO

Spicy chicken stew ▶

1 chicken, 1.2 kg/ 2 ½ lbs,
   ready-to-cook
1 head garlic
Cumin
Pimentón dulce
   (see page 12)
Boiled parsley potatoes
   (on the side)
Dry white wine
Vinegar
Coarse salt
Olive oil

Servings:	4
Preparation time:	15'+1h
Cooking time:	40'
Difficulty:	●●
Flavor:	●●
Kcal (per serving):	843
Proteins (per serving):	46
Fats (per serving):	52
Nutritional value:	●●

1 Singe the chicken, rinse it inside and out, and pat it dry. In the mortar, or blender, crush the peeled garlic, 2 tablespoons *pimentón*, and 3 teaspoons cumin to a paste. Transfer the paste to a bowl and dilute it with ½ glass vinegar and a few drops of wine. Rub the chicken with this paste, inside and out and set it aside for about 1 hour.

2 Cut the chicken into 10-12 pieces and brown in a terracotta pot with 5-6 tablespoons olive oil, turning frequently so they cook evenly. Add 1 glass wine, lower the flame, cover the pot and simmer for about 35 minutes. Check every now and then to make sure there is enough liquid, if necessary add a little hot water. Salt to taste. Serve the hot chicken with its sauce with *papas arrugadas,* or parsley potatoes on the side.

LAS CARAJACAS

Liver with savory sauce

600 gr/1 lb calf's liver,
   sliced
4 cloves garlic
4 slices fresh country bread,
   without the crust
3 hot red peppers
Red wine vinegar
Salt
Papas arrugadas (as the
   side dish, see page 75)

For the mojo:
1 head garlic
Cumin
Parsley
Salt
Olive oil

Servings:	4
Preparation time:	25'+3h
Cooking time:	10'
Difficulty:	●●
Flavor:	●●●
Kcal (per serving):	360
Proteins (per serving):	22
Fats (per serving):	15
Nutritional value:	●

Peel the head of garlic; in the mortar (or blender) reduce it to a paste with a sprig of parsley and ½ teaspoon cumin seeds. Put the paste into a bowl, blend in ½ glass olive oil and a pinch of salt. Place the liver slices into a large bowl without overlapping, and pour the mojo over them. Cover the bowl and refrigerate for 3 hours, turning the slices 2-3 times. Cook the liver in a dry skillet over a lively flame – 1 minute on each side. Slice it into strips and keep warm in the skillet.

Heat ½ glass olive oil in another skillet, brown the 4 peeled garlic cloves and the crumbled bread. After 4 minutes remove with a slotted spoon and save the oil in the skillet. Put the bread and garlic mixture into a mortar (or blender) with the washed, cut-up hot peppers and reduce to a paste. Put the paste back into the skillet with the oil, add 3 tablespoons vinegar and enough water to make a thick sauce. Pour this sauce over the liver, slowly heat the skillet until the sauce boils, salt to taste and serve immediately with *papas arrugadas.*

ROPA VIEJA CANARIA

Meat and vegetable stew

250 gr/8 oz lean beef
(preferably already boiled
or roasted)
250 gr/8 oz lean pork
(preferably already boiled
or roasted)
250 gr/8 oz dried chickpeas
10 *papas* (medium-small
potatoes)
1 onion
1 ripe tomato
1 yellow bell pepper
4 cloves garlic
1 fresh hot red pepper
Bay leaves, cumin
and thyme
Dry white wine
Black and green olives
(on the side)
Salt
Olive oil

Servings: 4	
Preparation time: 20'+6h	
Cooking time: 1h30'	
Difficulty: ● ●	
Flavor: ● ● ●	
Kcal (per serving): 516	
Proteins (per serving): 38	
Fats (per serving): 17	
Nutritional value: ● ●	

1 Six hours before you begin, put the chickpeas in cold water to soak. Wash the vegetables, remember to remove the seeds from the peppers and tomato and to peel the potatoes. Drain the chickpeas and put them into a stewpot with both meats. (If you are using uncooked meat, increase your quantities by about 2 ounces each). Cover with cold water, add pinch of salt and cover the pot. Bring to a gentle boil and cook for abut 1 hour, until the chickpeas are *al dente*. Remove the meat and chickpeas. Keep the cooking liquid.

2 Finely chop the onion and wilt it in an earthenware pot with 4 tablespoons olive oil; after 2 minutes add the whole, unpeeled cloves of garlic, 1 bay leaf, the leaves from 1 sprig of thyme, a pinch of cumin and the cut up hot pepper – without the seeds. Cook for 5 minutes then toss in the chopped tomato, the bell pepper, cut into strips, 1 glass wine and a pinch of salt, stir cook slowly for 5 minutes to reduce the sauce.

3 Cut the meats into strips, add it to the sauce along with the chickpeas and a couple of ladles of the hot broth. Bring the to boil and then simmer for 15 minutes – the sauce should be soupy.

4 In the meantime, brown the potatoes in skillet with a squiggle of oil, drain after 5 minutes and add to the stewpot 8 minutes before the cooking time is up. Garnish with bay leaves, parsley and thyme. Serve immediately with green and black olives on the side.

This recipe's name, that means "old dress", contains the secret of its origins. Like many other traditional foods, it is based on using leftovers (and specifically, puchero). A mainland dish, made with leftovers and eggplant, also has the same name. Add cooked chickpeas (or beans leftover from puchero, see page 23) to meat that has been cooking for 40 minutes, cook 20 minutes more. If you like, you can even add a sweet potato (see page 82).

SOLOMILLO AL PLÁTANO CANARIO

Banana tenderloin

1 Preheat the oven to 240°C/ 460°F Clean the vegetables; slice the tomatoes and remove the seeds. Tie the meat with kitchen twine to hold its shape, season lightly with salt and pepper. Grease a porcelain or earthenware oven pan with about half the lard, place the meat in it and cook in the oven for 10 minutes, turning so that it browns evenly.

2 Remove the pan from the over, add the sliced onion and carrot, cut into rounds, the sliced tomato and 2 peeled bananas, cut into circles as well, 1 bay leaf and a sprig of thyme. Put the pan back into the oven and lower the setting to 200°C/400 °C; roast for about 30 minutes, basting now and then with a little wine.

3 Remove the meat from the pan, put it on a serving platter to cool. Remove the twine and slice. Scrape the pan and put the drippings and bits into a saucepan. Bring to the boil over a low flame; cook for 3 minutes and then put the sauce through a fine strainer to remove the solid parts.

4 Put the strained sauce back into the saucepan, add the other two bananas – cut into circles and the remaining lard; let the flavors blend over a low flame. Serve the meat with the sauce and steamed rice on the side.

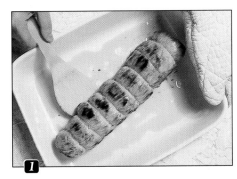

700 gr/ 1 ½ lbs beef tenderloin
4 bananas (ripe, but not brown)
1 onion
1 carrot
2 tomatoes
Bay leaves and thyme
2 dl /1 cup red wine
200 gr/8 oz steamed rice
Salt and pepper
50 gr/ 2 oz lard

Servings: 4	
Preparation time: 25'	
Cooking time: 1h	
Difficulty: ●●●	
Flavor: ●●	
Kcal (per serving): 705	
Proteins (per serving): 42	
Fats (per serving): 16	
Nutritional value: ●●●	

THE FISH

The beautiful coastal waters of the Canary Islands are home to many varieties of fish, and are visited by countless migrating species. And they have been the archipelago's "pantry" for ages. In addition to the species that thrive in other parts of the Atlantic and the Mediterranean such as gray mullet, conger eel, cod, moray eel, gilthead, bass and sole, there are anchovies, swordfish, sardines and mackerel, plus different varieties of tuna including bonito. There are wonderful octopus and calamari and other species related to what we find in our fish markets, or some that are native to the Canary Islands.

First of all, let us take a look at those featured in our recipes, the most popular varieties both fresh – or rather super-fresh to the joy of those lucky enough to taste them – and preserved.

In the Canary Islands cherne is a type of grouper, similar to polyprion americanus, the stone bass, that dwells in rocky depths. In mainland Spain (which the islanders call "the peninsula") they are known as cherna. If you cannot get the real thing, any type of grouper, halibut, cod or white fish will be fine. In the Islands, cherne like other abundant varieties is often preserved in salt to become the main ingredient of sancocho (see page 60). Guelde also known as longoron or guerde is an excellent Atlantic fish (atherina presbyter) which the mainlanders call pejerrey. In its stead we can use hake, small cod, mullet or other small white fish.

The famous sama, or sama dorada or sama de ley is nothing other than dentex (dentex dentex), denton in mainland Spanish. It favors sandy waters with rocks, like the besugo (pagellus acarne or aligote in Spanish), bocinegro (sparus pagrus pagrus, or sargus), breca or pagel (pagellus erythrinus, sea bream), corvina blanca (argyrosomus regius, meagre, a kind of umbra), chopa (spondyliosoma cantharus, sea bream), and herrera (lithognatus mormyrus, that is similar to striped bream). Sama de pluma (dentex filosus or gibbosus) related to dentex dentex is wonderful when grilled or baked under a coat of salt. You can readily use local dentex or porgy, or antoñito or dienton (dentex macrophthalmus or cachuco in Castilian Spanish), which is also similar to dentex.

Another fish that abounds in the waters and on the tables of the Canary Islands is mero, the big black grouper (epinephelus guaza) that likes rocky waters, like the islands' favorite, vieja (sparisoma creten-se) which is Spain is loro viejo. We can use sea bass, sea bream or similar fish. Other species that are plentiful in the rocky waters are abade or abae, (mycteroperca rubra, gitano in Spain), alfonsiño (beryx splendens), cabrilla (serranus atricauda, sea perch), catalufa (priacanthus cruentatus), salema (sarpa sarpa, similar to salpa); sargo (diplodus sargus cadenati, sargo marroquí in the homeland), a relative of white bream like sargo picudo that gets its name from the flattened nose, as well as rascacio or cantarero (scorpaena scropha, called cabracho in Spain, and scorpion fish in English. It is excellent in fish stews like boga (boops boops) and jurel (psuedocarnix dentex, also known as chicharro, which is the mainlanders' jurel denton).

We end this list with the oddest name of all, tapaculo which is a variety of turbot bothus podas maderensis, simply podas in Spanish, and any smooth turbot will be fine in the recipes.

On the sandy, muddy bottoms we find angelote (sguatina spp.), cazón (mustelus mustelus and galeorhinus gleus), chucho (dasyatis pasticana), raya (raya clavata, that is raya de clavos in Spain, and thornback ray fish in English), salmonetes, that is red mullet (mullus barbatus) along with surmullet (mullus surmuletus) called salmonete de roca or salmonete rayado in Spain) and torpedo (torpedo spp., electric ray and the Canary Islands cod (mora moro).

Among the favorite seafoods we cannot overlook lapa, a tender, tasty mollusk with a univalve shell, similar to the limpet, – but much bigger – that attaches to the rocks. It is stewed with garlic, parsley and wine, or baked with breadcrumb stuffing.

And there are other creatures populating the waters near the Islands that are a wonder to see rather than eat: the tortuga boba, a sea tortoise that basks on Tenerife's beaches, and further off the island's southern coast there is a colony of calderones, small whales also known as "blackfish."

PESCADOS

*The only problem with fish is making your choice –
the blue waters of the Atlantic Ocean contribute a
huge variety to the Islands' tables: cherne, mero,
sama, vieja that are cooked in a myriad of ways.
And there are delicious calamari and tender octopus.
The Canary Islands' seafoods, that are even better
when accompanied by the excellent local wines, are
wholesome and parsimonious. The ingredients are
simple and familiar, there is nothing strange or
extravagant and always a source of joy and pleasure
for the taste buds. The most famous and traditional
of all is sancocho an embodiment of Canary Island
cuisine that uses all the typical ingredients.
The recipes also explain which varieties of fish
you can use as viable substitutes.*

4

ALBÓNDIGAS DE PESCADO

Dentex fritters

1 Wash the half pepper, remove the seeds and rib; put it under the broiler, remove the skin and cut it into strips. Put the strips through the blender, set aside. Scald the fish fillets in lots of slightly salted boiling water; drain and reduce to a pulp in the blender. Set aside in a bowl.

2 Clean and finely chop the onions, wilt them in a skillet with 3 tablespoons olive oil. Drain and add to the fish along with the pepper paste, a sprig of chopped parsley and the egg; stir without beating. Then, blend in the juice of 1 lemon, 4 tablespoons tomato purée, 1 teaspoon *pimentón*, 4 tablespoons breadcrumbs and a pinch of salt.

3 Mix well, and then set aside for about 10 minutes. Take the batter and shape cherry-sized balls, dredge in breadcrumbs and fry in hot oil Remove them with a slotted spoon as they turn golden and drain on paper towels. Salt lightly.

4 In a shallow pan, dilute the rest of the tomato purée with a few drops of hot water, 3 tablespoons olive oil and 1/2 glass wine, add 1 bay leaf, the leaves from 1 sprig of thyme and the cleaned, crushed hot pepper. Bring the sauce to the boil and toss in the fritters, let them cook over a low flame and soak up the flavor for 6-7 minutes, turning occasionally. Garnish with lemon slices and parsley sprigs, and serve with boiled, parsley potatoes on the side.

			Servings: 4
600 gr/1 lb fillets of *sama* (or *cherne*, *mero* or similar fish, see page 50)	300 gr/12 oz tomato purée	Dry white wine	**Preparation time:** 30'+10'
2 onions	1 fresh, hot red pepper	Boiled *papas* (small potatoes, as the side dish)	**Cooking time:** 40'
1/2 bell pepper	*Pimentón dulce* (see page 12)	Salt	**Difficulty:** ●●
1 egg	Parsley (also for garnish)	Olive oil	**Flavor:** ●●●
2 lemons (one is for garnish)	Bay leaves or thyme	Oil for frying	**Kcal (per serving):** 624
	Breadcrumbs		**Proteins (per serving):** 31
			Fats (per serving): 36
			Nutritional value: ●●●

ATÚN EN ADOBO

Marinated tuna ▶

700 gr/ 1 1/2 lbs fresh tuna
   steak, 1 slice
1 head garlic
Pimentón dulce
   (see page 12)
1 fresh, hot red pepper
Bay leaves, oregano and
   thyme (also for garnish)
Parsley
   (for garnish)
Fried potatoes (side dish)
White wine vinegar
Salt
Olive oil

Servings: 4	
Preparation time: 20'+24h	
Cooking time: 20'	
Difficulty: ● ●	
Flavor: ● ● ●	
Kcal (per serving): 295	
Proteins (per serving): 37	
Fats (per serving): 15	
Nutritional value: ●	

Remove the skin and central bone from the tuna, cut it into slices or even, medium size strips. Put them in a bowl, without overlapping. Peel the garlic and in the mortar (or blender) reduce it to a paste. Transfer to a small bowl and mix in the finely chopped hot pepper – minus the seeds – 1 teaspoon *pimentón* and 1/2 glass olive oil; add 1 drop vinegar, one broken bay leaf, the leaves from a sprig of thyme, and a pinch each of oregano and salt. Spread this over the tuna, cover the bowl and refrigerate for 24 hours, turning the slices occasionally. Brown the fish in a skillet with 4 tablespoons olive oil and about 2 tablespoons of the marinade. Remove with a slotted spoon and drain on paper towels. In a small saucepan heat the rest of the marinade to just short of boiling. Arrange the fish on a serving platter, pour the hot marinade over it and serve with fried matchstick potatoes on the side.

CONGRIO CON ESCALDÓN

Conger eel with wheat meal

800 gr/ 1 3/4 lbs conger
   eel, sliced
12 *papas* (small potatoes)
200 gr/8 oz *gofio de trigo*
   (see page 15)
4 cloves garlic
Pimentón fuerte
   (see page 12)
Mojo verde (see page 14)
Saffron (1 sachet)
Salt and black peppercorns
Olive oil

Servings: 4	
Preparation time: 20'	
Cooking time: 20'	
Difficulty: ● ●	
Flavor: ● ●	
Kcal (per serving): 607	
Proteins (per serving): 44	
Fats (per serving): 17	
Nutritional value: ● ●	

Peel the potatoes (if they are small enough you can just wash them thoroughly) and put them in a pot with 1 1/2 liters (1 1/2 quarts) hot water, the peeled garlic 1/2 teaspoon *pimentón*, a pinch of salt, 6 peppercorns and 3 tablespoons olive oil. Bring to the boil, cover and cook for 10 minutes; add the cleaned eel and saffron; put the lid back on and boil for another 10 minutes. Remove the pot from the stove, take out the eel and potatoes, set aside and keep warm. Strain the cooking liquid and keep it boiling hot. Put the *gofio* into a bowl, add enough hot broth – stirring constantly – to make a thick meal (you can use the leftover broth for other dishes). Put the *escaldón* in individual bowls, dress with a little *mojo:* serve with the eel and potatoes, with additional *mojo* as the condiment.
This is a light, flavorful one-dish meal that is also delicious with other types of white fish. If you use more *gofio* and less water you can make *pella* – shape the *gofio* into a ball; slice and enjoy the pieces with *mojo*.

Calamares a lo Nina

Calamari with vegetables

1 Clean the onions, garlic and tomatoes – remove the seeds – and slice them all thinly. Gut the calamari and remove the ink sacs and outer membrane, then rinse them under cold running water, pat dry and cut them into pieces.

2 Use a saucepan (preferably terracotta) with a tight-fitting lid. Make one layer of calamari pieces, cover with the sliced onion, garlic and tomatoes.

3 Season with a pinch of salt and a dash of pepper, continue making layers in the same order as above until you have used all the ingredients (and remember to season each layer). Top with 1 bay leaf, a drop of vinegar and 8 tablespoons olive oil.

4 Cover, and cook over a low flame until it comes to a slow boil; there is no need to add water. Simmer for 40 minutes, check the salt and pepper. Sprinkle with the breadcrumbs and finely chopped parsley. Cook uncovered, over a medium flame for 5 minutes and serve immediately.

1 kg/2 lbs calamari
  (medium size)
4 ripe tomatoes
  (medium size)
2 onions
3 cloves garlic
Bay leaves and parsley
30 gr/1 oz breadcrumbs
White wine vinegar
Salt and pepper
Olive oil

Servings:	4
Preparation time:	25'
Cooking time:	50'
Difficulty:	● ●
Flavor:	● ●
Kcal (per serving):	354
Proteins (per serving):	33
Fats (per serving):	14
Nutritional value:	●

The tourist harbor at Los Gigantes on the island of Tenerife.

CALAMARES RELLENOS

Stuffed calamari

1 Rinse and dry the peppers, put the them under the broiler; remove the skins, seeds and ribs, cut them into strips and put them through the blender to make a paste. Clean and gut the calamari, remove the cartilage, eyes, beak; rinse and remove the outer membrane. Cut the lateral fins, separating them from the sacs, and chop finely with the tentacles.

2 Clean and finely chop the garlic and onions. In a bowl combine this with the pepper purée, the chopped fins and tentacles and a sprig of finely chopped parsley. Add a dash of salt and pepper. Set aside 3-4 tablespoons of the filling and use the rest to stuff the calamari. Secure them with a toothpick and sprinkle with a little flour.

3 Use a pan with a tight-fitting lid that is big enough to hold the calamari side by side (terracotta is preferable). Spread the "extra" filling on the bottom with a bay leaf, a pinch of saffron, $1/2$ glass wine and 6 tablespoons olive oil; mix and then put the calamari on top.

4 Slowly bring to the boil; cover and simmer for 40 minutes; add a little wine if it tends to dry. Five minutes before the cooking time is up, uncover to reduce the sauce. Remove from the stove, cool for a few minutes and serve garnished with bay leaves and chopped parsley.

Sparkling white houses in Puerto Mogán on Gran Canaria.

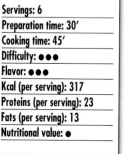

1 kg/ 2 lbs calamari
   (medium-small)
4 onions (medium-small)
2 bell peppers
1 head garlic
Bay leaves and parsley
   (also for garnish)
Saffron stigmas
Flour
Dry white wine
Salt and pepper
Olive oil

Servings: 6	
Preparation time: 30'	
Cooking time: 45'	
Difficulty: ●●●	
Flavor: ●●●	
Kcal (per serving): 317	
Proteins (per serving): 23	
Fats (per serving): 13	
Nutritional value: ●	

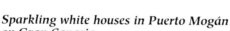

1 kg /2 lbs assorted stew fish (*boga, cantarero, jurel, mero, cod*, etc, see page 50), all ready to cook 2 onions 3 ripe tomatoes 2 bell peppers 4 cloves garlic	Bay leaves, parsley, thyme, saffron Salt and freshly ground pepper Vinegar Olive oil	
	Servings: 4	
	Preparation time: 20'	
	Cooking time: 30'	
	Difficulty: ●●	
	Flavor: ●●●	
	Kcal (per serving): 323	
	Proteins (per serving): 41	
	Fats (per serving): 13	
	Nutritional value: ●	

ENCEBOLLADO DE PESCADO

Fish and onion stew

1 The fish should all be "pot-ready", that is scaled, gutted, without heads, tails and fins, rinsed, dried and cut into pieces. Put all the pieces into a stewpot filled with lightly salted cold water and slowly bring to the boil. After 10 minutes, remove from the stove and drain the fish.

2 Clean and finely chop the onions, clean the peppers, remove the seeds and ribs and cut them into pieces; rinse the tomatoes, cut into pieces and remove the seeds. Slowly wilt the onions in a terracotta saucepan with 5 tablespoons olive oil, add the peppers, 1 bay leaf, a sprig each of parsley and thyme and a pinch of saffron. Then add the tomatoes.

3 While the tomatoes are slowly cooking, crush the peeled garlic in a mortar with a pinch of salt, a dash of freshly ground pepper and 1 teaspoon vinegar. Add this mixture to the saucepan; cook and stir for 2-3 minutes so the flavors can combine.

4 Now add the fish, bring to the boil and cook for another 6 minutes, stirring gently. Serve immediately.

MERO A LA NARANJA

Orange fish fillets ▶

700 gr/ 1 1/2 lbs *mero*
  fillets (see page 50)
2 oranges
4 cloves garlic
1/2 lemon
Parsley (for garnish)
Saffron stigmas
1 teaspoon *gofio de millo*
  (see page 15)
Salt
Olive oil

Servings: 4	
Preparation time: 30'	
Cooking time: 20'	
Difficulty: ● ●	
Flavor: ● ● ●	
Kcal (per serving): 279	
Proteins (per serving): 29	
Fats (per serving): 11	
Nutritional value: ●	

Toast a pinch of saffron stigmas in a dry skillet; chop and in a bowl combine them with the *gofio*, add a drop of lukewarm water and set aside. Lightly salt the fish fillets and sauté until golden with 6 tablespoons olive oil – about 2 minutes per side. Remove with a slotted spoon and drain on paper towels. Save the oil in the skillet. Arrange the fillets in a saucepan (terracotta would be best) and keep warm.

Peel and finely chop the garlic, slowly wilt it in the oil; slowly pour it over the fish in the saucepan. Add the juice of the 2 oranges and half the lemon. Bring to the boil; after five minutes add the saffron-*gofio* mixture and cook for 10 minutes more. Garnish with parsley sprigs and serve.

MORENA FRITA

Fried moray eel

800 gr/ 1 3/4 lbs moray eel
  slices
25 gr/1 oz *gofio de trigo*
  (see page 15)
1 lemon
Coriander leaves
  (for garnish)
Fried potatoes
  (as the side dish)
Salt
Oil for frying

Servings: 4	
Preparation time: 10'	
Cooking time: 20'	
Difficulty: ●	
Flavor: ● ●	
Kcal (per serving): 416	
Proteins (per serving): 37	
Fats (per serving): 26	
Nutritional value: ● ● ●	

Clean, rinse and dry the eel. Dredge the slices in the *gofio* (or flour). Fry in lots of hot oil; remove with a slotted spoon when they are a nice golden color. Drain on paper, salt lightly and garnish with lemon slices and coriander sprigs, and serve with fried potatoes.

Another classic way of preparing moray eel? Moisten 150 gr/6 oz bread – without the crust – with 3 tablespoons vinegar. Brown the slices in a skillet with olive oil, then sauté a nice bell pepper cut into rings. Put the eel into a pan, sprinkle with the bread, add 3 ladles of hot fish broth and the pepper rings. Slowly bring to the boil and cook for 10 minutes; serve the murena with papas arrugadas (see page 73).

PULPOS CANARIOS

Octopus with vinegar ▶

1 Clean the octopus, turn out the sac to gut, remove the beak and eyes. Rinse thoroughly and cut it into chunks and rub them with salt. Peel and thinly slice the garlic and onions. Remove excess salt from the octopus and put the pieces into a heavy saucepan with a lid (preferably terracotta) along with the garlic and onion, add 1 tablespoons vinegar and enough cold water to cover it all.

2 Cover the saucepan, and over a very low flame, gently bring to the boil; skim and add 1 glass wine. Cover and simmer for about 45 minutes. Remove from the stove and let the octopus pieces cool in the liquid, they should be tender. Drain and serve on a platter with a generous sprinkling of chopped parsley and sliced boiled potatoes, or even better *papas arrugadas* (see page 75).

SARDINAS CON TOMATE

Sardines with tomatoes

1 kg/ 2 lbs fresh sardines
3 ripe tomatoes
1 small onion
2 cloves garlic
Dry white wine
Parsley (for garnish)
Salt
Olive oil

Servings: 4	
Preparation time: 20'	
Cooking time: 20'	
Difficulty: ●●	
Flavor: ●●	
Kcal (per serving): 420	
Proteins (per serving): 34	
Fats (per serving): 21	
Nutritional value: ●	

Clean and gut the sardines, cut off the heads. Rinse under cold running water and pat dry. Cook them in a skillet (2 minutes per side) with 6 tablespoons olive oil, remove with a slotted spoon and keep warm. Wash and finely chop the tomatoes. Finely chop the onion and garlic, and sauté them in the same skillet; add the tomatoes and simmer gently for 10 minutes. Add the sardines and $1/2$ glass wine. Boil for 5 minutes, and then serve with a sprinkling of chopped parsley. In the Islands, sardines are also fried crisp – either with breadcrumbs or just flour – and served with an aromatic *mojo*.

1 kg/ 2 lbs octopus (medium-small)	*Papas arrugadas* (as the side dish, see page 75)	**Cooking time:** 45'+20'
2 medium onions	Vinegar	**Difficulty:** ●●
3 cloves garlic	Olive oil	**Flavor:** ●●
Parsley		**Kcal (per serving):** 308
Dry white wine	**Servings:** 4	**Proteins (per serving):** 28
Coarse salt	**Preparation time:** 20'	**Fats (per serving):** 2
		Nutritional value: ●

EL SANCOCHO

Fish with potatoes and salsa ▶

700 gr/ 1 ¹/₂ lbs *cherne salado* fillets
(see page 50)
600 gr/1 lb *papas*
(medium-small potatoes)
2 cloves garlic – or 1 small onion

For the mojo:
6-8 cloves garlic
1 dried hot red pepper
Cumin
Pimentón dulce
(see page 12)
Salt
Vinegar

Servings:	4-6
Preparation time:	20'+24h
Cooking time:	20'
Difficulty:	●●
Flavor:	●●●
Kcal (per serving):	208
Proteins (per serving):	26
Fats (per serving):	1
Nutritional value:	●

1 The day before you prepare this dish, soak the fish in cold water – and change the water several times to remove the salt. Peel the potatoes. If you are using new potatoes, just rinse them thoroughly. Unless they are very small, cut them into circles. Put them into a filled pot with cold water, 2 peeled garlic cloves, cover and boil for 10 minutes. Add the *cherne* fillets, lower the flame and simmer for 10 more minutes. Drain the fish and potatoes, put them on a platter and keep warm. Keep the cooking liquid.

2 In the mortar (or blender) crush the remaining garlic (peeled of course), with a pinch of salt, the hot pepper (remember to remove the seeds!), a pinch of cumin seeds and 1 tablespoon *pimentón*. Put the mixture into a bowl, mix in 2 tablespoons vinegar and 2-3 pieces of boiled potato – crushed with a fork – and enough of the cooking liquid to make a soft, but not watery sauce. Serve the fish and potatoes with a light coating of *mojo,* and put the rest in a sauceboat.

VIEJAS ENCEBOLLADAS

Fish with onions

4 *viejas*, about 250 gr/8 oz
each (see page 50)
2 onions
1 ripe tomatoes
1 green pepper
3 colves garlic
Pimentón fuerte
(see page 12)
Bar leaves, parsley
and thyme
20 gr/1 oz breadcrumbs
Papas arrugadas
(as the side dish,
see page 75)

Servings:	4
Preparation time:	20'
Cooking time:	30'
Difficulty:	●●
Flavor:	●●●
Kcal (per serving):	340
Proteins (per serving):	42
Fats (per serving):	11
Nutritional value:	●

Wash and clean the vegetables as customary. Clean, scale, rins and dry the fish. Brown the fish in a pan with 8 tablespoon olive oil, cooking about 3 minutes on each side. Remove with a slot ted spoon, drain and keep warm. Chop the onion and wilt it slowly i the same pan, after 5 minutes add the cut-up green pepper, 1 bay lea a sprig each of parsley and thyme and then the chopped tomat While this is cooking slowly, in the mortar combine the peeled garli with a teaspoon of *pimentón* and reduce to a paste; add this to sauc that is cooking. Stir and after a couple of minutes add the *viejas* wit the breadcrumbs and a glass of hot water; salt to taste. Cover, bring t the boil, then simmer for 7 minutes and serve with *papas arrugadas.*

If you cannot find the salted fish that purists consider indispensable you can use fresh, white fish fillets such as branzino, grouper, cod, etc., and adjust the amount of salt accordingly. Like all traditional recipes, this one, too, has many variations. Some people cook the fish – with onions instead of garlic – separately from the potatoes; many add batatas (see page 82), that is sweet potatoes, and generally the amarilla variety and serve the sancocho with a pella de gofio (see page 15), that they blend with the remaining cooking liquid. And, if you like, you can embellish the mojo with parsley and olive oil.

SAMA CON BERROS

Dentex with watercress

1 kg/ 2 lbs dentex
   (1 whole fish,
   see page 50)
150 gr/6 oz watercress
   (1 bunch)
1 onion
3 cloves garlic
Flour
Dry white wine
Papas arrugadas
   (as the side dish,
   see page 75)
Salt and pepper
Olive oil

Servings: 4
Preparation time: 30'
Cooking time: 30'
Difficulty: ●
Flavor: ● ●
Kcal (per serving): 382
Proteins (per serving): 37
Fats (per serving): 17
Nutritional value: ● ●

Gut and scale the fish, remove the fins, head and tail. Cut it into thick slices, salt them lightly, put them on a platter and sprinkle with a little flour. Clean the vegetables; wash the watercress and chop it very finely. Chop the onion and garlic and wilt in a skillet with 3 tablespoons olive oil. Set aside and keep warm. Arrange the fish slices in a pan without overlapping, brown them in 5 tablespoons olive oil, turn after 3 minutes, add $^1/_2$ glass wine and let it evaporate over a high flame.

Add the sautéed garlic and onion, the chopped watercress and a pinch each of salt and pepper and $^1/_2$ liter/ 2 cups very hot water. Bring to the boil and cook over a medium flame for about 15 minutes. Serve with *papas arrugadas*.

Huevos
y verduras

Like all Spanish peoples, the inhabitants of the
archipelago which is known as the "Seven Jewels"
share a fondness for tortillas. Here we will also enjoy
recipes that use the excellent vegetables and legumes
of the Islands. When meat was not as common as it
is today, eggs nourished generations of islanders.
Above all, in this chapter we will meet the
archipelago's most famous food: papas arrugadas
that hide a refined and gentle soul under a rough
skin. And since they owe their inimitable flavor to the
land where they grow, to the ocean's salt and fire –
they seem to reflect the nature of the place itself –
volcanic islands bathed by the blue waters – where
any time is the best time to enjoy them.

5

TORTILLAS CANARIAS

Vegetable omelets

8 eggs
3 ripe tomatoes
1 onion
1 clove garlic
Basil and parsley
Salt
Olive oil

Servings: 4	
Preparation time: 20'	
Cooking time: 30'	
Difficulty: ●●	
Flavor: ●●●	
Kcal (per serving): 408	
Proteins (per serving): 23	
Fats (per serving): 30	
Nutritional value: ●●	

1 First wash and clean the vegetables and herbs. Chop the onion finely and wilt it in a skillet with 3 tablespoons olive oil. After 5 minutes add the chopped garlic.

2 Chop the tomatoes and add them to the skillet along with a pinch of salt and a sprig each of chopped parsley and basil; let the flavors combine over a low flame for about 10 minutes.

3 Beat 2 eggs with a pinch of salt; grease a pan with a few drops of olive oil, when it is hot pour in the eggs; as soon as the eggs have set, add one quarter of the vegetable mixture, fold in half so that the edges meet; finish cooking the omelet. Remove from the skillet and set aside in a warm place. Repeat until you have used up all the eggs and filling. Serve.

Folk dancers and musicians entertaining visitors, in Pueblo Canario on Las Palmas.

This is just one – and one of the most popular – of the many tortillas you can enjoy in the Islands – made with peppers, papas and batatas (see page 82), berros and green beans, as well as different types of cheeses. There are also sweet, cinnamon flavored tortillas made with the delicious plátano canario (and comparing them to just any banana is practically an insult) or the sugared gofio and papas tortillas.

3

GARBANZOS COMPUESTOS

250 gr/8 oz dried chickpeas
3 eggs
40 gr/ 1 $^1/_2$ oz shelled
  almonds
30 gr/ 1 oz raisins
2 liters/2 quarts vegetable
  broth
1.5 dl/ $^1/_2$ cup milk
Dry white wine
Salt

Servings: 4
Preparation time: 15'+6h
Cooking time: 1h30'
Difficulty: ●●
Flavor: ●●
Kcal (per serving): 566
Proteins (per serving): 30
Fats (per serving): 24
Nutritional value: ●●

Stewed chickpeas ▶

Before you begin, soak the chickpeas for 6 hours. When you are ready, drain them and put them in a saucepan (preferably terracotta), with the broth and a pinch of salt. Cover and boil gently for one hour. In the meantime, soak the raisins in a glass of wine. Hard cook the eggs (about 7 minutes from when the water boils), shell, let cool and slice them into circles. Scald the almonds in boiling water for 5 minutes. Drain, peel and grind finely. Squeeze out the raisins. In a saucepan combine the raisins, the egg slices and milk, as soon as it starts to boil, turn off the flame. Remove the chickpeas from the stove, drain and put them back in the pot. Add the egg and milk mixture, stir, cook slowly for five minutes to combine the flavors and serve.

EL ESCACHO

400 gr/14 oz *papas*
  (medium size potatoes)
250 gr/8 oz *gofio
  de mezcla* (see page 15)
1 green onion
4 fresh, hot green peppers
4 cloves garlic
60 gr/ 2 oz *queso palmero*,
  aged and grated
  (see page 78)
Cumin
Vinegar
Salt
Olive oil

Servings: 4
Preparation time: 20'
Cooking time: 15'
Difficulty: ●
Flavor: ●●●
Kcal (per serving): 448
Proteins (per serving): 13
Fats (per serving): 15
Nutritional value: ●

Potato loaf

Clean the onion and hot peppers; peel the potatoes and scald them in lightly salted boiling water for 15 minutes – during the last 5 minutes add the onion cut into chunks. In the meantime, use the mortar (or blender) to make a paste of the peppers, peeled garlic and a pinch of cumin seeds. Put the paste into a mixing bowl, add 8 tablespoons olive oil, 2 tablespoons vinegar, the cheese and a pinch of salt. Mix. Drain the potatoes, saving the liquid. Chop the potatoes and onion, and add to the bowl, mixing well. Gradually add the *gofio,* and enough of the hot cooking liquid to make it firm enough to shape into a ball. Serve with any dish, soup or fish. And if you want to go all the way, you can mix in some *chicharrones,* crispy, golden pork rind, or crumbled bacon strips.

JUDÍAS A LA VINAGRETA

Beans with vinegar dressing

250 gr/8 oz dried
    white beans
2 eggs
1 green onion
1 ripe tomato
2 fresh hot green peppers
2 cloves garlic
Bay leaves and oregano
Parsley (also for garnish)
Vinegar
Salt and pepper
Olive oil

Servings:	4
Preparation time:	20'+5h
Cooking time:	1h
Difficulty:	●
Flavor:	●●
Kcal (per serving):	363
Proteins (per serving):	20
Fats (per serving):	16
Nutritional value:	●

Soak the beans in advance for 5 hours. Drain, and put them in a saucepan (terracotta would be best) . Cover with cold water, add a pinch of salt and 1 bay leaf. Put on the lid and slowly bring to the boil; cook for 1 hour. In the meantime, hard cook the eggs (7 minutes from when the water boils), shell them, cool and slice in circles. Clean and wash the vegetables, remember to remove the seeds from the tomato and peppers. When the beans are done, drain and put them into a salad bowl with the onion – cut into little rings, the peppers in strips, the tomato in chucks and the egg slices. Peel the garlic, in the mortar reduced it to a paste and blend in a pinch of oregano, a sprig of chopped parsley and a dash of pepper with oil and vinegar. Dress the salad and toss. Sprinkle with chopped parsley just before serving.

PAPAS ARRUGADAS

Salted potatoes

The true *papas arrugadas* are new, or small potatoes that are boiled in seawater. We, however, will use normal tap water with lots of salt (1 tablespoon salt for every liter/quart of water). Boil the potatoes in their jackets until they are *al dente*, drain well and put them in an oven dish. Bake at 220° C/425° F for 12 minutes. The heat will crinkle the skins all, and in fact, *arrugadas* means "wrinkled." Serve immediately with Canary Islands foods, or with any other meat or fish dishes. Or, do as the locals do, and enjoy them alone – or better – with lots of *mojo picón* (see page 12).

If there is no oven, drain the potatoes, put them back in the pot and dry them over a hot stove, moving them with a wooden spoon until they lose all the excess water and the skins wrinkle. If you use bigger potatoes, you will need to cook them longer.

600 gr/1 lb *papas* (medium-small potatoes) Sea salt	

Servings:	4
Preparation time:	5′
Cooking time:	30′
Difficulty:	●
Flavor:	● ●
Kcal (per serving):	130
Proteins (per serving):	4
Fats (per serving):	0
Nutritional value:	●

TOMATES AL ESTILO DE LAS PALMAS

Stuffed tomatoes

1 Clean the poultry breast, removing any little bones, cartilage or fat. Brown quickly, on both sides in 2 tablespoons olive oil. Drain well and put it through the blender with the ham to make a smooth paste.

2 Rinse the tomatoes, remove the stems, cut them in half horizontally, scoop out the pulp with the seeds. Fill each half with the chicken (or turkey) and ham mixture, press down, and make each one a little dome.

3 In a mixing bowl combine the breadcrumbs, chopped parsley, a dash of pepper, just a tiny bit of salt and 1 tablespoon, olive oil. Set the oven to 200° C/400° F.

4 Spread the breadcrumb mixture over the stuffed tomatoes evenly. Grease an oven dish with a squiggle of olive oil, arrange the tomatoes side-by-side and bake for 15 minutes. Let them cool to lukewarm, and garnish with parsley before serving. They are also very good eaten cold!

4 ripe, firm tomatoes
150 gr/6 oz chicken (or turkey) breast
150 gr/6 oz lean cured ham (1 thick slice)
Parsley (also for garnish)
80 gr/3 oz breadcrumbs
Salt and pepper
Olive oil

Servings: 4-6	
Preparation time: 20'	
Cooking time: 20'	
Difficulty: ● ●	
Flavor: ● ●	
Kcal (per serving): 495	
Proteins (per serving): 18	
Fats (per serving): 34	
Nutritional value: ● ● ●	

The dunes of Maspalomas on Gran Canaria.

THE CHEESES

The Canary Islands, where animal raising is still a major source of income, are famous for their excellent cheeses made according to the traditional methods. The raw goat's milk cheeses, such as majorera and palmera (from the Islands' fine breeds), have earned denomination of origin (denominación de origin) labels, the European recognition of quality. Not only are the queso majorero and queso palmero renowned for their for tradition and quality, they have outstanding nutritional value!

Queso majorero, pride of the Island of Fuerteventura is made in the areas of Antigua, Betancuria, La Oliva, Pájara, Puerto del Rosario and Tuineje. It is a fat, semi-pressed cheese made from the wonderful raw milk of the majorera goat - when it is to be aged, not more than 15% sheep milk is added – usually from animal rennet (made from dried kid stomach). After the curd is broken, and crumbled to grains that vary in size according to the aging, the cheese is put into moulds, salted (usually dry with sea salt, or in brine) and aged in well-ventilated darkened rooms. There are three types, the tierno (fresh, ripened from 8 to 20 days), semicurado (ripened 20 to 60 days) and curado (aged more than 60 days). The cheeses are flat wheels, not more than 35 cm (14 inches) in diameter, and weigh from 1 to 6 kg (2 to 13 pounds). The rind, which is nothing more than a pale veil on the tierno cheese, gets darker and thicker on the riper varieties. It is marked with an imprint of the original pleita, palm fronds. The paste is compact with tiny holes – or none at all – and creamy with a slightly sharp taste. The color ranges from white to ivory in the riper cheeses, and the flavor, becomes, more distinct and slightly salty with an aroma of goat milk in the riper cheeses. They can be seasoned with pimentón (see page 12), olive oil or gofio (see page 15), so the appearance and flavor change accordingly. The animal raising tradition, that dates back to the native peoples, is truly ancient on the island of La Palma, which is famous for its rich pastures that offer fresh forage all year long. The excellent queso palmero is made from the fine raw (that is, not pasteurized) milk of the local goats with natural kid rennet. These cylindrical wheels can weigh as much as 15 kg (33 pounds). The paste is pressed, and dry-salted with sea salt. This cheese is usually eaten fresh, with its mild flavor, but there are also tierno, semicurado, curado, and above all, ahumado varieties. The ahumado is smoked over aromatic fires that burn pine bark and needles, as well as almond shells, that give the impalpable white rind a grayish tone. This cheese too can be dressed with olive oil or dusted with gofio. The Canary Islands also make other cheeses, from ewe's and cow's milk or combinations of the two, they may be raw or pasteurized, ripened to varying degrees, oiled, greased or smoked, with flavors that vary according to aging and finishing processes. Each island has its own specialty. There is pressed, raw queso gomero from the La Gomera, made of raw goat's and ewe's milk. The cheeses weigh from 1 to 1.5 kg (2 to 3 pounds), with a smooth, hard, ochre colored, oily looking rind, compact, yellow flaky paste. Generally aged or smoked it has a distinctive, slightly spicy flavor with a hint of burnt wood. Although cheeses made from goat's milk prevail on Gran Canaria, there are others too. The island's specialty is queso de flor. It comes from the high ground between Gula and Galdar, and is made from pasteurized cow and sheep milk, or sometimes even goat milk), with vegetable rennet from thistles that gives the cheese its name. It is pressed, uncooked, into cylinders with rounded edges and available in fat and semi-fat, wheels, weighing from 500 grams to 2.5 kg (1 to 5.5 lbs). The rind starts out thin and white, and becomes yellowish, smooth and waxy in the riper varieties, like the paste that changes from creamy to hard with a smooth grain and a slight bitter finish. The cheese known as queso de media flor is made with vegetable and animal rennet. San Mateo is another famous cheese from Gran Canaria, fat and semi-fat, with a pressed paste made from pasteurized goat, sheep and cow milk. It is made in several varieties: fresh, with or without salt, tierno, semicurado (aged for 30 days) and curado (aged for 5 months). Similarly to the processes and traditions of the other islands, only the goat milk cheeses are aged, the others ripen within a short time. Nor is there a lack of full and semi-fat, uncooked pressed cheeses on the other islands: queso herreño from El Hierro, made from raw or pasteurized cow's, ewe's or goat's milk is often smoked. The color and flavor vary according to the prevailing milk; it has tiny holes and a lively flavor when aged. White, queso lanzaroteño from Lanzarote is eaten fresh, it is made from whole, raw or pasteurized goat's milk in moulds weighing from 1 to 4 kg (2 to 9 lbs). The thin rind is imprinted with the woven palm frond. The white, creamy, compact paste, with little salt has a pleasant, slightly sour flavor and delicate aroma. The rind gets thicker, and the flavor becomes sharper in the semifrescos, semicurados and curados varieties. The island of Tenerife also boasts fresh goat's milk cheeses with a pleasant, slightly sour flavor, and the smoked and mixed-milk varieties are no less delicious.

Postres

And, we will end on a sweet note. It is space
that prevents us from presenting all the wonderful
traditional desserts and pastries from the Islands.
We have opted for the most famous and favorite
selections that emphasize the genuine spirit
of the archipelago's foods. These desserts can be
called humble miracles. With the magic of anise
and lemon they transform the simplest and most
familiar ingredients – milk, flour, cheese,
fruit and honey – into pure poetry, leaving aside
swirls of whipped cream, chocolate curls and
other frills without any regrets at all.

6

BIEN-ME-SABE

Coconut custard

3 whole eggs, and 4 yolks
500 gr/1 lb sugar
18 dry biscuits
 (like ladyfingers)
Ground cinnamon
1 coconut with the milk

Servings: 6	
Preparation time: 20'	
Cooking time: 20'	
Difficulty: ●	
Kcal (per serving): 913	
Proteins (per serving): 19	
Fats (per serving): 42	
Nutritional value: ●●●	

1 Open the coconut, extract the milk. Remove the flesh. In a saucepan combine the sugar and 1 glass water. Heat slowly, mixing all the while until you get a clear syrup. Remove the pan from the stove and let it cool to lukewarm, then blend in the coconut milk. Heat again, over a low flame until it just boils. Set aside to cool.

2 In a bowl beat the eggs and yolks until creamy.

3 Pour the beaten eggs into a saucepan, blend in the lukewarm syrup, one tablespoon at a time, stirring after each addition. Heat the custard very slowly and remove it from the stove the instant it starts to boil.

4 Arrange the biscuits on the bottom of a flat pan, without overlapping, cover with the cream. Smooth the top and sprinkle generously with ground cinnamon. Serve chilled, decorated with strips of fresh coconut.

A vacation village on Tenerife.

BUÑUELOS DE BATATAS

Sweet potato fritters ▶

4 *batatas* (sweet potatoes)
30 gr/ 1 oz sugar
Sweet wine
   (raisin wine)
Dry white wine
1 lemon
30 gr/ 1 oz flour, plus some
   for your worktable
Milk
Salt
Oil for frying

Servings: 4-6
Preparation time: 25'
Cooking time: 35'
Difficulty: ●●
Kcal (per serving): 533
Proteins (per serving): 6
Fats (per serving): 27
Nutritional value: ●●●

1 Cook the sweet potatoes in their jackets in boiling, slightly salted water for 15 minutes. Drain, peel and mash them. In a mixing bowl, combine the potatoes with 1 glass sweet wine, 1/2 glass dry wine, the lemon juice, flour and sugar. If the mixture is too thick, dilute with a drop or two of cold milk.

2 Take a tablespoon of the mixture, and with your hands shape it into a "date", put it on your floured worktable, or on a clean cloth. Repeat until you have used up all the mixture. Fry a few *buñuelos* at a time in hot oil, remove when golden and drain. Serve them hot – but they are also good cold.

The sweet potato (ipomoea batatas) comes from South America, and is a convolvulacea. The ivory colored pulp has a delicate flavor that is not at all sugary. The pulp, rich in carbohydrates, vitamins and minerals, is enclosed in a skin that ranges from yellow to light brown. It is also called camote from the ancient Nahuati language, or boniato – originally boniata – a name that may have its roots in the Antilles. It is an American species that is widely grown in Brazil and Cuba and is now also cultivated in Florida.

BOLLOS DE LECHE

Milk rolls

400 gr/14 oz flour
   (plus extra for the
   worktable
   and baking pan)
2.5 dl / 1 cup milk
120 gr/ 4 oz sugar
1 egg
Anise seeds and ground
   cinnamon
Grated zest of 1/2 lemon
20 gr/1 oz brewer's yeast
25 gr/1 oz lard
70 gr / 2 1/2 oz butter

Servings: 6-8
Preparation time: 30'+3h
Cooking time: 35'
Difficulty: ●●
Kcal (per serving): 505
Proteins (per serving): 9
Fats (per serving): 20
Nutritional value: ●●●

Heat the milk to lukewarm. Pour the flour into a mound on your worktable; make a well in the middle; dissolve the yeast in a little milk, and delicately combine it with the flour. Knead the dough, gradually adding the rest of the milk as you work. Shape the dough into a ball, cover and set aside to rise in a warm, but not hot, place for 1 hour. Knead again, adding the sugar, 2 oz of the butter, the lard, grated lemon zest, and a pinch each of anise seeds and cinnamon. Cover the dough, and set aside for 1 hour. Knead again, to "loosen" the dough, and make little balls. Arrange them side by side in a buttered, floured baking pan, cover with a cloth and set aside to rise for the third and final time. In the meantime, preheat the oven to 180° C/350°F. Bake for 35 minutes.

Bollos, a specialty of the island of La Gomera are wonderful with afternoon tea, or as a snack. Milk is the main ingredient in many of the Islands' desserts such as custards, lemon and cinnamon flavored cuajada that includes dry biscuits, or leche asada, that you will read about further on.

83

Frangollo, *which is not to be confused with gofio is also very popular in Argentina. It is coarsely ground cornmeal (and you can even find bits or even whole kernels in it). In its stead you can use cornmeal for polenta. Some people mix the frangollo with wheat or other types of flour. Or, you can use half* frangollo *and half blanched almonds ground together with dried figs. This traditional Island dessert can also be served simply sprinkled with sugar.*

FRANGOLLO

◀ Sweet cornbread

For the frangollo:
500 gr/1 *frangollo*
  (see opposite page)
Sugar (for garnish)
Zest of 1 lemon
2 sticks cinnamon
Palm honey

For the flavored milk:
1/2 liter/1 pint milk
20 gr/1 oz sugar
Zest of 1/2 lemon
1 stick cinnamon

Servings: 6
Preparation time: 10'
Cooking time: 1h
Difficulty: ● ●
Kcal (per serving): 370
Proteins (per serving): 10
Fats (per serving): 5
Nutritional value: ● ● ●

1 In a large, preferably terracotta, saucepan combine 1/2 liter/ 1 pint water, lemon zest and cinnamon. When it boils, remove the lemon and cinnamon, and gradually pour in the *frangollo* stirring constantly with a wooden spoon. Continue cooking, and stirring, over a medium flame. If the *frangollo* starts to dry out, add a little hot water. Cook for about 30 minutes or until the *frangollo* comes away from the sides of the pot in a single mass. Turn it onto a cutting board and cool. Slice and serve with palm honey and flavored milk.

2 While the *frangollo* is cooling, heat the milk over a low flame together with the lemon zest cut into pieces and the cinnamon, stirring constantly. When it boils, lower the flame and keep on cooking and stirring for about 10 minutes. Remove the lemon and cinnamon, add the sugar and boil for another 15 minutes. Pour into a bowl, cool and serve with the *frangollo*.

GOFIO DE ALMENDRAS

Almond terrine

500 gr/1 lb *gofio*
  de mezcla (see page 15)
100 gr/4 oz cane honey
150 gr/6 oz shelled almonds
Dry white wine
Grated zest of 1/2 lemon
Anise seeds
Ground cinnamon
40 gr/ 1 1/2 oz lard

Servings: 4-6
Preparation time: 15'
Cooking time: 30'
Difficulty: ● ●
Kcal (per serving): 756
Proteins (per serving): 16
Fats (per serving): 27
Nutritional value: ● ● ●

Toast the almonds in a dry skillet. Peel and grind 100 gr /4 oz, set the rest aside. Put the almonds back in the pan, add the grated lemon zest and continuing toasting and stirring; be careful not to let the mixture burn. After 5 minutes add 1 glass wine, bring to the boil, then lower the flame and cook for 5 minutes more. Gradually blend in the *gofio,* lard, honey and a pinch each of anise seeds and cinnamon. When the mixture starts to thicken, remove it from the stove, turn into a bowl, and decorate with the almonds you had set aside. Cool before serving. You can also pour it into pretty little moulds, or serve it sliced.

Rapadura *are similar, and they are made with the same ingredients: gofio, honey, almonds, sugar, anise, cinnamon and lemon. The mixture is poured into buttered cone-shaped moulds and chilled until firm.*

LECHE ASADA

Milk and honey pudding ▶

1 liter/1 quart milk
6 eggs
70 gr/ 2 1/2 oz sugar
Ground cinnamon
Grated zest of 1 lemon
15 g/ 1/2 oz cornstarch
Palm honey
(for garnish)

Servings: 4
Preparation time: 30'
Cooking time: 30'
Difficulty: ● ●
Kcal (per serving): 490
Proteins (per serving): 25
Fats (per serving): 22
Nutritional value: ● ● ●

Preheat the oven to 180° C/350° F. Heat the milk to lukewarm over a low flame; remove the saucepan from the stove and take 1 glass of the milk – set the rest aside. Dissolve the cornstarch in the glass. In a mixing bowl, beat the eggs with a spoon, blend in the sugar, the diluted cornstarch and the rest of the milk; add the grated lemon zest and 1/2 teaspoon cinnamon. Pour the mixture into a pudding mold – without a central hole. Bake for 20 minutes, or until a knife inserted into the middle comes out clean. Turn the pudding onto a serving plate and serve with a bowl of palm honey on the side.

PAN DULCE DE LOS ALTOS DE TEJEDA

Anise loaf

500 gr/1 lb flour (plus some for the baking pan)
4 eggs
150 gr/6 oz sugar
Grated zest of 1/2 lemon
15 gr/1/2 oz cornstarch
Anise seeds
60 gr/ 2 oz butter

Servings: 4-6
Preparation time: 10'
Cooking time: 1h
Difficulty: ● ●
Kcal (per serving): 678
Proteins (per serving): 20
Fats (per serving): 21
Nutritional value: ● ● ●

Preheat the oven to 180° C/350° F. In a saucepan combine the eggs, sugar and finely grated lemon zest. Cook over a low flame (or in a double boiler), stirring with a wire whisk until creamy. Gradually add the cornstarch, flour and a pinch of anise seeds, stirring constantly, blend in about two thirds of the butter, until the mixture is smooth. Pour into a slightly buttered and floured loaf pan. Bake for 40 minutes. When the *pan dulce* has cooled, enjoy it with honey or jam; or have it for breakfast – dunking it into a glass of milk.

If you cannot find palm honey, you can use cane honey (or molasses), or regular honey. There are several variations on this dessert, including a famous one from Tenerife that calls for adding 100 gr/4 oz blanched, finely ground almonds (the other quantities remain the same). Boil the milk with 1 tablespoon butter, cornstarch, cinnamon and lemon zest. Strain and blend in the slightly beaten eggs and sugar. Add the ground almonds and then bake. On Guamasa, instead of the almonds they use 6-8 crumbed plain biscuits and garnish the finished dessert with grated coconut.

PESTIÑOS

◀Fried triangles

I n the mortar crush the anise seeds to a paste; combine with 2 tablespoons each of milk, olive oil and wine. In a bowl combine the sugar, flour and a pinch of salt. Add the anise seed mixture and mix – adding a little water if needed – to make a smooth dough. Set aside for 30 minutes. Work the dough again to "loosen" it, roll it out thinly on the floured worktable. Use a knife, or cookie-cutter to make triangles that measure 4-5 cm (1 1/2-2 inches) on a side. Fry in hot oil, drain and dry on paper papers. Cool to room temperature and serve.

350 gr/13 oz flour
  (plus some for your
  worktable)
20 gr/1/2 oz anise seeds
15 gr/1 oz sugar
Milk
Dry white wine
Salt
Oil for frying
Olive oil

Servings: 4	
Preparation time: 30'+30'	
Cooking time: 20'	
Difficulty: ●●	
Kcal (per serving): 713	
Proteins (per serving): 8	
Fats (per serving): 37	
Nutritional value: ●●●	

TORTA DE BATATAS

Sweet potato cake

P eel the apples and the *batatas*. Put them in a large pot and cover with water. Cover the pot, bring to a gentle boil and continue cooking this way for 20 minutes. Preheat the oven to 200° C/400° F. Drain the potatoes and apples, and slice them into circles. Use one pat of butter to grease a baking pan, and make a layer of slices, sprinkle with sugar and a hint of cinnamon; continue making layers until you have used up the ingredients. Sprinkle the last layer with the breadcrumbs and then melt the remaining butter and pour it over the top. Bake for 20 minutes. Serve the cake lukewarm with a sprinkling of cinnamon.

800 gr/ 1 3/4 lbs *batatas*
  (sweet potatoes)
3 apples
120 gr/4 oz sugar
30 gr/1 oz breadcrumbs
Ground cinnamon
100 gr/4 oz butter

Servings: 6-8	
Preparation time: 20'	
Cooking time: 40'	
Difficulty: ●●	
Kcal (per serving): 369	
Proteins (per serving): 4	
Fats (per serving): 15	
Nutritional value: ●●●	

TORTITAS DE PLÁTANO

Banana fritters ▶

4 *plátanas canarias*
  (see page 92)
3 eggs
100 gr/4 oz flour
1 dl / ¹/₂ cup milk
10 gr/ ¹/₂ oz baking
  powder
Ground cinnamon
Grated zest of ¹/₂ lemon
Rum
Honey
  (for topping)
Oil for frying

Servings: 4	
Preparation time: 20'+30'	
Cooking time: 20'	
Difficulty: ●●	
Kcal (per serving): 799	
Proteins (per serving): 11	
Fats (per serving): 31	
Nutritional value: ●●●	

P eel the bananas, put them through the blender or mash with a fork. Put the mashed bananas into a bowl, and using a wire whisk blend in the eggs, milk, salt, ¹/₂ teaspoon cinnamon and the grated lemon zest. When the mixture is smooth, add the baking powder, flour and a small glass of rum. Set the batter aside to rest for 30 minutes, then, drop a tablespoon at a time into the hot oil and fry until golden. Drain on paper towels and serve with a little honey on top (if the honey is too thick, you can dilute it with a little lukewarm water).

TRUCHAS DE QUESO

Cheese dumplings

500 gr/1 lb *queso tierno*
  (see page 78)
400 gr/14 oz flour
  (plus some for
the worktable)
1 egg white
20 gr/1 oz sugar
Anise seeds
Confectioners' sugar
  (for topping)
Salt
40 gr/ 1 ¹/₂ oz lard
Oil for frying

Servings: 4-6	
Preparation time: 30'+30'	
Cooking time: 20'	
Difficulty: ●●●	
Kcal (per serving): 1080	
Proteins (per serving): 39	
Fats (per serving): 65	
Nutritional value: ●●●	

M ound the flour on the floured worktable: add the egg white and lard (or softened butter), ¹/₂ teaspoon crushed anise seeds, and a pinch of salt. Knead and add enough lukewarm water to make a smooth, firm dough. Set aside for 30 minutes. Soften the *queso* with a fork, blend in the sugar. Knead the dough a little more to soften it and roll it out. Use a round cookie-cutter or cup to make discs about 12 cm (about 4 ¹/₂ to 5 inches) in diameter. Knead the scraps together, roll out and cut more discs until you have used up all the dough. Put a little of the cheese mixture in the middle of each disc. Fold in half, moisten edges and press down with the tines of a fork to seal. Fry a few *truchas* at a time in hot oil – remove with a slotted spoon when they are nicely golden. Drain on paper towels. Arrange them on a platter and when they are lukewarm, dust with a sprinkling of confectioners' sugar.

As an alternative to **queso tierno** *you can use grated hard, or semi-hard paste* *cheese as long as it is not too ripe and mix it with the sugar.*

TREASURES OF THE HESPERIDES AND GIFTS OF BACCHUS

The fruits of the Hesperides

It was no accident that the ancients "placed" the mythical garden of the Hesperides on these islands with their magnificent climate and fertile soil. The Canary Islands are indeed a lush, green paradise. La Palma, Gran Canaria, Tenerife and to a lesser extent La Gomera, offer not only countless vegetables, that include several varieties of papas (the local name for potatoes), batatas (sweet potatoes), delicious tomatoes but also the grains and legumes – as we have seen on page 15 – for the essential gofio. Citrus fruits and almonds ripen to perfection in the orchards, and plump, golden grapes droop on the vines (in the section about wines we will also talk about the islands of Lanzarote and El Hierro that are also famous for their figs). In addition to supporting the typical vegetation of temperate zones, so that harvests last almost all year long, the archipelago's soil and climate are perfect for palms and sugar cane (that we will get back to) and even coffee. But the prize crops are exotic fruits, tender avocado, juicy pineapple, delicate guava, mango and fragrant papaya, and now there are developing plantations of litchi, carambola and other fruits.

The most outstanding – in quality and quantity – fruit of the Canary Islands is, however, the exquisite plátano, symbol of the archipelago's wondrous relationship with nature. They are far tastier than the bigger bananas generally eaten in Europe and America. The plátano is a species exclusive to the Canary Islands (probably a derivation of the species musa cavendishii*), that is rich in minerals (iron, phosphorous, magnesium, manganese, copper and mainly potassium which among other virtues, helps absorb solar radiation). It is a complete food since it also contains large amounts of healthful fiber and A, B, C and E vitamins. Anyone who is lucky enough to taste a plátano on the Canary Islands, picked ripe and eaten on the spot will certainly appreciate the difference with respect to our "common" bananas that generally ripen in some cargo hold rather than on the tree. Plátanos do, however, travel well, as the consumers in Spain and Portugal who prefer them will gladly attest. Its firm pulp is perfect for cooking – fried or in one of the recipes we present here – and yields much better results than the plantains, the big South American bananas that have a flavor more like a potato or squash. Finally, in addition to being delicious and nutritious, the plátano has other healthful, "external" uses. Not everyone knows that the skin of the ripe fruit is a fine remedy for corns and warts. And the substances in the pulp provide excellent protection against the sun, like another plant which, thanks to the extraordinary local climate, develops its properties to the full: aloe.*

The Wines

The archipelago produces excellent white, rosé and red table as well as sweet dessert wines that have been celebrated by Shakespeare, Goldoni and Lord Byron. The output is not huge, but the quality is good and improving constantly. They are generous, varietal or blended wines, made mainly from local grapes that ripen on the sun-drenched volcanic land and often at surprising altitudes (up to 1700 meters or 5777 feet!). In spite of the scarce precipitation, it is the hygroscopic power of volcanic soil and specifically the layer of ash and lapillus known as picón that permits grape-growing in extreme conditions. During the night it absorbs the moisture, known as "horizontal rain" carried by the trade winds and conserves it throughout the long, sun-filled days. Obviously, the grape growers had to develop original techniques – that vary from island to island – to adapt to these unusual conditions, and they often required enormous effort. The dry, cool air, especially in the uplands, provides the advantage doing away with the need for chemical treatments and this greatly benefits the wines.

The most common grapes are the red and white Listán; other white grapes are Gual, Marmajuelo, Verdello, Vijariego, and the aromatic Malvasia and Muscatel. The prevalent red grapes are Negramoll and Tintilla. Lively, whites, that can even be quite strong, are the most widespread wines, but there are good rosés and robust, full-bodied young

reds that often improve with age. The sweet and fortified wines are outstanding, and sparkling varieties have recently joined the ranks. Grapes are usually harvested between late August and the end of October. Winemaking and refining techniques are evolving and more and more land is being dedicated to vineyards.

The Canary Islands' wines already have eight D.o.c. designations, five of which are from Tenerife (Abona, Tacoronte-Acentejo, Valle de Güímar, Valle de La Orotava and Ycoden-Daute-Isora), the others bear the names of their island homes: El Hierro, Lanzarote and La Palma.

As fitting, we will start with Tenerife, cradle of the archipelago's wines, where Abona is located. The area, known for its excellent white wines is situated on the southern slope of the Island. The vineyards, are planted mainly between 400 and 800 meters, on porous volcanic soil, and rise up to the 1700 meters of Vilaflor where the soil is clayey and fertile. But grape growing at those altitudes requires enormous experience and special techniques. The pleasing white wines (minimum alcohol content 10.5%) are flanked by the rosés (11%) and reds (11.5%), and the "after-dinner" varieties, dulce clásico, made from Malvasia or Muscatel grapes and de licor (both 15%), with the latter more of a liqueur to which alcohol is added.

Perhaps the most renowned name from Tenerife is Tacoronte-Acentejo famous for reds that can be refined and aged, and other, strong wines that are made according to a strict, detailed discipline that excludes "harsh" treatments. The production zone, located on the northern slope of the Cordillera Dorsal comprises the municipalities of Tegueste, Tacoronte, El Sauzal, La Matanza de Acentejo, La Victoria de Acentejo, Santa Ursula, La Laguna, El Rosario and Santa Cruz de Tenerife, with the sub-zone of Anaga that corresponds to the area of Parque Rural de Anaga in the municipalities of La Laguna, Santa Cruz de Tenerife and Tegueste. It is an enchanting, terraced slope, covered with green grapevines, that rises from the sea to a height of 1000 meters (3000 feet), with most of the vineyards between 300 and 750 meters. The cultivation technique is quite original. To get the most from the sun, the vines are planted in rows 6-8 meters (20-26) feet apart, the

long shoots are arranged in rays held by supports known as horquetas. This not only facilitates harvesting, it also leaves room for other crops, such as potatoes.

The young reds with their unique, intense fruited aroma and marked flavor include tinto tradicional (12-13.5%). It is a lovely bright cherry red with purplish overtones, with a hint of red fruits in the bouquet and dry, balanced, slightly tannic taste with good structure. The tinto maceración (12-12.5%) is made by packing the grapes in hermetically sealed containers for a week. Then they are gently squeezed. The wine, with its bright cherry color and marked purplish edge has a hint of raspberry and currant in the bouquet. On the palate it reveals body, balance and persistence with an elegant

tannic finish. Then there is the full-bodied tinto barrica (12-13%), aged for 6 months in oak barriques (225 liters - nearly 50 gallons) with a pleasing woody fragrance, and full, vigorous, persistent flavor; the tinto crianza, aged at least 6 months in barriques and 18 in the bottle, and the tinto reservas (12 months in barriques and 24 in the bottle), wines with a complex bouquet with touches of dried and fresh fruits, wood, tobacco and vanilla. The clear, bright, purplish pink rosado (12.5%) is made mainly from dark Listán grapes that are briefly macerated on the must and fermented under controlled conditions at 18°C. This wine has an intense, fruity bouquet with touches of pineapple and strawberry, and full, fresh, persistent flavor, with good body.

The range of white wines, produced by gentle squeezing and in lesser quantities, includes the pale blanco seco with a good structure (with alcohol content from a minimum of 10% to 11.5 -12%), fermented at low temperatures (17°C/62.6°F) to enhance the fruity bouquet that varies according to the blend, with floral and anise notes, a lively, full and elegant flavor.

There is also the semiseco (12%) fermented at 16°C/60.8°F, with an intense, fine floral bouquet, delicate and balanced flavor, and the blanco barrica (12-12.5%) that is aged in barriques for 2 months, a fine fruity bouquet with touches of citrus and wood, a full palate with hints of oak that blend well with the fruity tones, it has an excellent structure and perfect balance. The heading blanco tradicional (13% to as high as 16%) covers wines made and bottled exclusively in the Anaga sub-zone. The color is sometimes rosy because it is traditionally made from red and white grapes. The sweet wines include Malvasia clásico made from Malvasia grapes that are overripe from either late harvesting or lots of sun, and the de licor variety (both have an alcohol content of 15%).

Next on our survey are the Valle de Güímar wines, that get their name from the rift valley located on the southeastern side of Tenerife. The production zone with its rather steep slopes above 500 meters includes the areas of Arafo, Candelaria and Güímar, where grapes grow between 600 and 800 meters and even dare to go beyond 1600 meters! Dry and lightly sweet whites prevail. They are fine and elegant, made to be enjoyed young (10% minimum alcohol content, but generally

between 11 and 12%), made from Listán grapes with small amounts of Gual, Muscatel and Vijariego, that are pressed gently and fermented at low temperatures. The blanco barrica is aged in oak barriques. It is a fresh, complex wine with a balanced fruity bouquet that includes hints of wood. The purplish-pink rosado (10.5%) is made mainly from Listán grapes that are briefly fermented on the must at 16°C. It has an intense bouquet with a touch of berries and a full, fresh flavor.

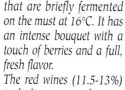

The red wines (11.5-13%) include varieties that are made by carbonic maceration like Beaujolais and Italian vino novello – with a purplish color, intensely fruity bouquet with notes of raspberry and currant. The cherry red tinto jóven has an equally rich flavor; the grapes are macerated briefly prior to pressing. The robust tinto barrica has a structured, persistent taste, and it is made with a longer maceration process and aged in barriques for 6 months. The local list is rounded off with dulce clásico made from overripe Malvasia or Muscatel grapes, with excellent varietal fragrances and structured, persistent flavor; the de licor (both have an alcohol content of 15%), and the recent addition to the family, a sparkling wine (11%) made from white Listán grapes, that is bottle fermented according to the classic method; straw yellow in color with pale green highlights, a lively, fine sparkle and varietal bouquet with hints of yeast and a delicate flavor.

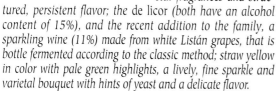

On the northern slope of the Cordillera Dorsal of Tenerife is the beautiful Valle de La Orotava, lush with fields and vineyards. It is known for its delicate wines – the exposure is the key – of the same denomination. They include flavorful whites and elegant, light reds. The production zone, on a gentle slope covers the municipalities of La Orotava, Los Realejos and Puerto de la Cruz. The vineyards are located at altitudes from 400 to 800 meters, in the medianias with its loose, rocky, fertile volcanic soil. The vineyards are often arranged in original, complex ways, such as La Perdoma with its entwined cordons. The range includes whites (11%), rosés (11%) and reds (11.5%) that can be aged, as well as dulce clasico and de licor (both 15%) made from pure, overripe Malvasia or Muscatel grapes, and the sparkling wine made with the classic method. Our overview of Tenerife will end with the Ycoden-Daute-Isora that is dedicated to quality wines. The

historic nucleus of the production zone - located on the northwest corner of the island and exposed to ocean breezes on two sides – is the area of Icod de los Vinos. It has been famous ever since the Canary Islands were a compulsory stop for ships traveling between the Old and New Worlds in the XVI and XVII centuries – and the famous "Canary Wine" shipped from the port of Garachico was the main source of revenue. The name is inspired by the Islands' earliest inhabitants, the Guanche, when the Menceyatos or kingdoms of Ycoden and Daute prospered under Princess Isora. The production zone includes the areas of San Juan de la Rambla, La Guancha, Icod de los Vinos, Garachico, Los Silos, Buenavista del Norte, El Tanque, Santiago del Teide and Guía de Isora. The espalier vineyards are located mainly between 200 and 800 meters above sea level, but there are some as low as 50 and as high as 1400, they are terraced because the steep slopes hinder the use of machinery.

On this rough and rocky terrain, soil is mainly volcanic with ashes and rock, it is light, fertile and well-drained. Rainfall is somewhat greater than on the other islands: summer droughts are compensated by the trade winds. The area produces dry white, straw color white wines (minimum 11%: but the semi-sweet, barrica and blanco crianza varieties can be as strong as 14%), aromatic, strawberry color rosés (11.5%, but the barrica reaches 14%), lively, fresh, balanced, flavorful reds (12-14%) The color is a ruby red with purplish tones when young, fruity notes, a good structure and therefore, good for aging. The list of reds also includes those made by carbonic maceration, tinto tradicional and crianza that are aged extensively in barriques. And, of course, though produced in limited quantities there are the sweet Malvasia and Muscatel wines (14-22%).

Moving on to the other islands, El Hierro that is lacking in springs and waterways owes its prosperity to its vineyards that are scattered over steep terraces at altitudes from 200 to 700 meters, and the hygroscopic nature of picón. White grapes predominate (Listán and Vijariego, which here is called Verijadiego or Diego, along with Bermejuela known as Bremajuelo, Gual, Malvais and Verdello). The red grapes are dominated by Listán (known as Negramuelle), Mulata (Negramoll) and Bastardo (Baboso). The rich white wines (11%) have vigor and character; the rosés (11.5%) are fresh and fruity, while the reds (12%) are full-bodied and warm to the palate. The dulce clásico, made from aromatic grapes, never has less than 14% alcohol, and the de licor ranges from 15 to 22%.

On Lanzarote, the easternmost island in the archipelago, white wines, prevail slightly over the reds. The production zone is practically the whole island, with its hills and volcanic cones, and encompasses the areas of Tinajo, Yiza, San Bartolomé, Haría and Teguise. The extremely dry, but mild climate, is negatively affected by the hot winds blowing in from nearby Africa. This means that tiring cultivation techniques are a necessity. Planting a vine means digging large, inverted cone shaped holes by hand, in the volcanic blanket that covers the land from depths of 20 cm to 20 meters; then 70 cm high semicircular dry-walls have to be built – by hand – to protect the young shoots from the burning Saharan winds. The production range includes dry white whites (10.5%), with hints of yellow, exotic fruits, like the lightly sweet wines, a sweet, amber Muscatel and the pale Diego (12.5-14%), the local name for Vijariego. In addition to rosés (11-14%), the island also produces flowery, spicy reds (11%), and a large among of dulce clásico, since Malvasia grapes abound, as well as de licor (both have alcohol contents of 15%). There is also espumoso, a classic-method sparkling wine made with at least 85% Malvasia or Muscatel and some authorized white grapes (15-22%).

Talking about Malvasia is like mentioning La Palma, dominated by the Caldera de Taburiente, cradle of the aromatic grape that came from the Orient and has a Greek name. On the deep, steep and fertile mineral rich soil, the exceptionally long-lived vines that were introduced by the Portuguese grow at heights from 200 to 1200 meters. The production zone that extends over most of the island's perimeter is divided into three sub-zones. There is Fuencaliente-Las Mancas, the home of Malvasia, in the southwestern part where there has been recent volcanic activity, with vines planted up to the edges of the lava flow on ground covered by pícon or large stones; Hoyo del Mazo-Las Breñas, on the eastern side of the island where mainly red grapes are grown on stony soil; and Zona Norte-Vinos de Tea, on the northern curve where tiny, tree-shaded vineyards produce original resinated wines that age for six months in Tea pine (pinus canariensis) barrels.

The production range includes delicate white wines (11-14.5% alcohol content). They are mainly varietal, fresh and light, mild rosés (11-13%), made from Negramoll fermented off-skin and the ruby reds (11-13%), also mainly varietal. The resinated Tea wines (11-13%) made from Negramoll and Albillo are a soft cherry-red with brick nuances. The bouquet is fruity and grassy with a marked resiny finish. But finest and most famous nectars from the island are the aromatic, golden and amber sweet wines made from grapes such as Sabro, Gual, Verdello (15-22%) and mainly, a step above the others – the sublime Malvasia (that once grew throughout the archipelago before it was struck by phylloxera – made in the clásico (15-22%) and dry (14-16%) varieties from overripe grapes.

Sugar cane and rum

On the Canary Islands, the gentle climate and fertile soil, especially at sea level, are perfect for raising sugar cane. And so, in addition to a myriad of traditional liqueurs made from a variety of substances such as honey, palm and fruits (originally made by natural fermentation) the Islands produce an excellent rum, which, as we know is made from molasses the thick liquid by-product of

sugar manufacturing. Canary rum is different from the pale and light variety made in the former Spanish Antilles – Dominican Republic, Cuba, Puerto Rico and the Virgin Islands, and from the dark strong liquor from Jamaica, Barbados and Demerara in Guyana.

No one actually knows the origins of the word "rum". It may be a corruption of the acronym RVM (Rectificando Veram Medicinam meaning – distill it and you will obtain medicine) selected in 1480 by a Benedictine monk in Erfurt as the name for the precious elixir he made that would delight aristocratic palates in small doses and then became – according to those who uphold the legend – rum with a vowel, hence the Castilian ron – the rough drink of pirates. Others maintain that rum, also known as kill-devil was rumbullion a Devonshire work for "ruckus", abbreviated into rum, but no one can confirm it. What is certain is that in 1667 the fine spirits made from sugar cane were already known as rum or ron.

In the Canary Islands, systematic sugar cane farming (the plant comes from the Far East and was brought to the West by the Portuguese) dates from when the archipelago became a Castilian dominion, XVI-XVI century. Sugar production brought the islands huge benefits. It was from here that the cane was taken to Santo Domingo and in the New World found the perfect environment for sugar and molasses production that would soon outstrip the Canary Islands. American competition, helped by the use of slaves, led to the ruin of the Canary Islands' plantations. So, they began distilling molasses in the archipelago, creating a liquor that soon became popular. In the late XVII century distilleries of various types began to spring up throughout the islands, especially in the monasteries. But once again American competition, mainly from New England made itself felt. Production then turned to alkermes colored with cochineal and this became an important source of income in the mid-eighteenth century, that is when the Germans discovered anilines. Sugar cane enjoyed a rebirth and once again the Islands were covered with plantations. In 1884 a modern plant for making excellent rum and sugar was opened at Arucas on Gran Canaria, and its products soon became famous throughout the world. The juice of

the cane – that ripens about one year after planting, around February – called guarapo is extracted and fermented with substances that each producer keeps secret, and then distilled – usually twice. The distillate ages in oak casks, it is the wood that darkens the color, for anywhere from one to fourteen years. Then caramel may be added before bottling. At the historic Arucas distillery there is now a museum that conserves a magnificent collection of rum from all over the world.